There's a

MIRACLE

in Your

MOUTH

E. W. Kenyon &
Don Gossett

WHITAKER
HOUSE

There's a Miracle in Your Mouth

Don Gossett
P.O. Box 2
Blaine, Washington 98231
www.dongossett.com

ISBN: 978-1-60374-092-0
Printed in the United States of America
© 2009 by Don Gossett

Whitaker House
1030 Hunt Valley Circle
New Kensington, PA 15068
www.whitakerhouse.com

3 4 5 6 7 8 9 10 **W** 16 15 14 13 12

Contents

Overcoming Fear and Difficulty

Finances and Stewardship

Praise, Love, and Prayer

Introduction

Christianity is often called "The Great Confession." All things in Christ—salvation, healing, deliverance—are dependent upon the confession with our lips of Jesus' lordship. Paul said to Timothy, *"You...have confessed the good confession in the presence of many witnesses"* (1 Timothy 6:12).

Throughout this book, you will find great confessions that God honors. For maximum results in applying the principles of this book in your own life, you may wish to read these great confessions aloud. When doing so, personalize the Scriptures by quoting them in the first person, applying them directly to your life's circumstances.

So then faith comes by hearing, and hearing by the word of God. (Romans 10:17)

The Power
of Speaking God's Word

Believing and Confessing the Word

L iving in God's power means living in the spirit of faith. What is the spirit of faith? The apostle Paul defined the spirit of faith with a quotation from Psalm 116:10, "*I believed, therefore I spoke,*" saying, "*Since we have the same spirit of faith, according to what is written, 'I believed and therefore I spoke,' we also believe and therefore speak*" (2 Corinthians 4:13).

The spirit of faith is something we have, something we possess. We are faith men and faith women. The Bible makes it clear that God has given to everyone "*a measure of faith*" (Romans 12:3). As Christians, we are not a host of doubters, but we have been born into "*the household of faith*" (Galatians 6:10).

The spirit of faith is similar to the word of faith, as defined in Romans 10:8: "'*The word is near you, in your mouth and in your heart*' (that is, the word of faith which we preach)." The true faith life is a mouth and heart experience. It is believing the Word in your heart and speaking or confessing the Word with your mouth.

Exercise the Spirit of Faith

We invariably speak what we believe, whether it is right or wrong. Jesus taught, *"Out of the abundance of the heart the mouth speaks"* (Matthew 12:34). When we exercise the true spirit of faith, we believe the Word and then speak that Word.

We believe the Word in Ephesians 1:7: *"In Him we have redemption through His blood, the forgiveness of sins, according to the riches of His grace."* Therefore, we speak, "I am redeemed from the kingdom of darkness through the precious blood of Jesus."

We believe the Word in 1 John 2:25: *"This is the promise that He has promised us; eternal life."* Therefore, we speak, "I have eternal life according to His great promise."

We believe the Word in Matthew 28:20: *"I am with you always, even to the end of the age."* Therefore, we speak, "The Lord is with me always, even until the very end of life's journey."

We believe the Word in Hebrews 11:16: *"God is not ashamed to be called their God, for He has prepared a city for them."* Therefore, we speak, "God is my God, and He has prepared for me a beautiful city."

We believe the Word in Proverbs 11:25: *"The generous soul will be made rich, and he who waters will also be watered himself."* Therefore, we speak, "The Lord is prospering and watering my life, for by His grace I am a generous and cheerful giver."

We believe the Word in Jude 24: "*Now to Him who is able to keep you from stumbling, and to present you faultless before the presence of His glory with exceeding joy.*" Therefore, we speak, "The Lord will keep me from falling and will present me faultless before His presence."

The person with the spirit of faith has the confession: "I have the spirit of faith. I believe the Word; therefore, as I speak it, I am a member of the household of faith. God has given to me '*a measure of faith.*' I never speak of doubt, for I am a believer. The Word is near me, in my heart and in my mouth. Through the word of faith, I am a victor, because faith is the victory!"

Speak Success, Not Failure

Declare the new creation, not the old. Speak it: "I am a new creature in Christ Jesus; the old things have passed away, and all things have become new." (See 2 Corinthians 5:17.)

Speak your righteousness in Christ, not unworthiness. Affirm it: "I am the righteousness of God in Christ Jesus." (See 2 Corinthians 5:21.) Speak the language of the new kingdom of God's dear Son in which you now dwell, not the old kingdom of darkness from which you have been saved.

Giving thanks to the Father who has qualified us to be partakers of the inheritance of the saints in the light. He has delivered us from the power of darkness and conveyed us into the kingdom of the Son of His love, in whom we have redemption through His blood, the for-giveness of sins.   (Colossians 1:12–14)

Speak that you are an heir of God and a joint heir with Jesus Christ, not your old identity as a captive to sin and Satan. Testify to it: "I have a rich inheritance. I am blessed with every spiritual blessing. The Father Himself loves me." (See Ephesians 1:3; Romans 8:17.)

Speak that you have the life of God in your mortal body, not the old spirit of inferiority, failure, and frustration. In Christ, *"we live and move and have our being"* (Acts 17:28).

Speak healing and health, not how sick and diseased you are. Isaiah 33:24 foretells a future time when *"the inhabitant will not say, 'I am sick.'"* That's a good practice in kingdom living. Don't say, "I am sick," but speak the Word that heals: "With His stripes, I am healed." (See Isaiah 53:5.)

Speak financial success, not poverty and misery. Speak marital success, not marriage failure. *"Then you will make your way prosperous, and then you will have good success"* (Joshua 1:8).

Words That Win

Someone once told me, "I have nothing left but words, empty words, dead words. I am broke. Everything is gone."

I looked at him and said, "How did you make your money?"

"I made it selling goods."

"Haven't you the same kind of words now that you had then?" I asked.

He said, "I have the same words, but there is nothing in them anymore."

"What did you have in your words that made them turn to money?"

"I had fire; I had youth; I had ambition."

"Have you lost all that?"

"Yes, and more."

Then I said, "Did you ever meet the man called Jesus?"

"Never, sir," he answered.

"You know nothing about Him, then?"

"I have heard preachers talk about Him. The other night, I heard a fellow on the street talking about Him."

"But if I should tell you this morning that this Jesus could put back into you this fire and zeal, give you love, and give you a place in the world better than you lost, wouldn't that cause you to be interested in Him?"

"If He could do that for me, I would go across the continent on my knees."

"You don't need to do that. He is here in the room. He has heard me talking about Him. He has heard what you have said. If you will take Him as your Savior and Lord, victory will be yours again. He rejuvenates dead, worn-out hopes. He restores lost faith. He makes the voice vibrant again. He gives back lost health. He creates new opportunities. He gives the ability to have success. Do you want to take Him?"

"It's worth the chance—I have nothing to lose. I have all to gain. I'll take Him!"

Right Confessions

Jesus said, *"For by your words you will be justified, and by your words you will be condemned"*
(Matthew 12:37).

Words That Justify and Words That Condemn

You are justified when you say, as God's Word
says, *"As far as the east is from the west, so far has He
removed our transgressions from us"* (Psalm 103:12).
But you are condemned if you say, "The Lord holds
the sins of my youth against me."

You are justified when you say, as God's Word
says, *"No evil shall befall you, nor shall any plague
come near your dwelling"* (Psalm 91:10). But you are
condemned if you say, "I am afraid, and I don't feel
safe."

You are justified when you say, as God's Word says,
*"He who is in you is greater than he who is in the
world"* (1 John 4:4). But you are condemned if you
say, "The power of the devil is just too much for me."

You are justified when you say, as God's Word says, "*They will lay hands on the sick, and they will recover*" (Mark 16:18). But you are condemned if you say, "I'm getting worse."

You are justified when you say, as God's Word says, "*With long life I will satisfy him*" (Psalm 91:16). But you are condemned if you say, "I'm going to die; I won't live long."

You are justified when you say, as God's Word says, "*Bless the LORD, O my soul…who heals all your diseases*" (Psalm 103:2–3). But you are condemned if you say, "I just can't receive healing from some of my diseases."

You are justified when you say, as God's Word says, "*Your healing shall spring forth speedily*" (Isaiah 58:8). But you are condemned if you say, "I just can't enjoy the blessing of divine health."

We can condemn ourselves by our own words. The results of this are not pleasant. But, as the Scripture says, "*Happy is he who does not condemn himself in what he approves*" (Romans 14:22). If we are not under condemnation, then we can possess great confidence toward God.

> *Beloved, if our heart does not condemn us, we have confidence toward God. And whatever we ask we receive from Him, because we keep His commandments and do those things that are pleasing in His sight.* (1 John 3:21–22)

Walking with God by Agreeing with Him

We cannot truly walk with God unless we agree with Him. *"Can two walk together, unless they are agreed?"* (Amos 3:3). To agree with God is to say the same thing God says in His Word about salvation, healing, prayer, and living an overcoming life.

First of all, we agree with God by saying that we are who God says we are—His children, new creatures in Christ. We say also that we are *"more than conquerors"* through Christ (Romans 8:37). We disagree with the devil, who would try to convince us that we are no good, failures, or weaklings.

How can we walk with God in power, blessing, and usefulness? By agreeing with God that we have what He says we have: His name, His nature, His power, His authority, and His love. We agree that we have what God says in His Word that we have.

Just as Enoch *"walked with God"* (Genesis 5:22), so we can walk with God by agreeing that we have received the ability to do what He says we can do: witness with power, cast out demons, and minister His healing power. *"I can do all things through Christ who strengthens me"* (Philippians 4:13). We agree that we can do what God says in His Word that we can do.

If we speak only what our senses dictate, we will not be agreeing with God. It is through speaking the Word that we agree with God. It is the confession of faith that is our victory. To walk with God, we must disagree with the devil, as Jesus did, by boldly declaring, "It is written that He resisted the devil. I can, too." (See, for example, Matthew 4:1–11.)

You can walk with God daily by agreeing with Him and His Word. Because He has said it, we may boldly say it, too. (See Hebrews 13:5–6.)

You Will Possess What You Confess

Your confession of faith precedes your possession of what you are desiring and seeking.

Confess Jesus as Lord (see Romans 10:9–10), and you will possess salvation.

Confess that "*by His stripes we are healed*" (Isaiah 53:5), and you will possess healing.

Confess that the Son has made you free (see John 8:36), and you will possess absolute freedom.

Confess that "*the love of God has been poured out in our hearts by the Holy Spirit*" (Romans 5:5), and you will possess the ability to love everyone.

Confess that "*the righteous are bold as a lion*" (Proverbs 28:1), and you will possess lionhearted boldness in spiritual warfare.

Confess that God "*will never leave you nor forsake you*" (Hebrews 13:5), and you will possess the presence of God with each step you take.

Confess that you are the redeemed of the Lord (see Psalm 107:2; Revelation 5:9), and you will possess redemption benefits every day.

Confess that "*the anointing which you have received from* [God] *abides in you*" (1 John 2:27), and your "*yoke will be destroyed because of the anointing*" (Isaiah 10:27).

Confess that in the name of Jesus you can cast out demons (see Mark 16:17), and you will possess dynamic deliverances over Satan's power.

Confess that "*they will lay hands on the sick, and they will recover*" (Mark 16:18), and you will possess healings for the oppressed.

Confess that you are a branch of the living Vine (see John 15:5), and you will possess Vine life wherever you go.

Confess that you are "*the righteousness of God in Him*" (2 Corinthians 5:21), and you will possess the ability to stand freely in God's holy presence, and in Satan's presence as a victor.

Confess that you are "*the temple of the living God*" (2 Corinthians 6:16), and you will possess the reality of God dwelling in you and walking in you.

Confess that "*God shall supply all your need according to His riches in glory by Christ Jesus*" (Philippians 4:19), and you will possess God's supply for your every need.

We May Boldly Say

As we launch out in bold Bible living, learning to confess God's Word in the midst of all our situations, we need to see exactly why we have the right to make these confessions.

We know that we have the right to boldly confess God's Word because of Hebrews 13:5–6: *"For He Himself has said, 'I will never leave you nor forsake you.' So we may boldly say: 'The Lord is my helper.'"* Notice that it is because of what *"He Himself has said"* that *"we may boldly say."*

Because He has said, *"I am the LORD who heals you"* (Exodus 15:26), we may boldly say, "Yes, Lord, I am in health because You are the Lord who heals me."

Because He has said, *"Whoever offers praise glorifies Me"* (Psalm 50:23), we may boldly say, "I am glorifying my Creator by praising Him."

Because He has said, *"Man shall not live by bread alone, but by every word that proceeds from the mouth of God"* (Matthew 4:4), we may boldly say, "I have esteemed Your Word more than my necessary food." (See Job 23:12.)

Let no thoughts dwell in your mind that contradict what He has said. You just boldly say the same thing.

God says of His own Word, "*I am the Lord. I speak, and the word which I speak will come to pass....The word which I speak will be done*" (Ezekiel 12:25, 28). You can count on God's Word being good. It cannot fail without God failing. The Lord has also said,

> So shall My word be that goes forth from My mouth; it shall not return to Me void, but it shall accomplish what I please, and it shall prosper in the thing for which I sent it.
> (Isaiah 55:11)

The following sections are all part of God's Word, which He has sent forth to accomplish His purposes. Because He has said these things, we may boldly say them, knowing the Lord will accomplish the purpose of His Word. Because He has spoken, we know that we can declare it boldly. It will be as He has said because "*there has not failed one word of all His good promise, which He promised*" (1 Kings 8:56).

We may boldly say, "God is for us."

Because He has said, "I have come that they may have life, and that they may have it more abundantly" (John 10:10), we may boldly say, "I have that abundant life in me now because I have received Jesus Christ as Lord."

22

Because He has said, "*If God is for us, who can be against us?*" (Romans 8:31), we may boldly say, "God is for me, and no one can succeed against me."

Because He has said, "*Whoever confesses Me before men, him I will also confess before My Father who is in heaven*" (Matthew 10:32), we may boldly say, "Jesus is confessing me right now before the Father because I am confessing Him before men."

Because He has said, "*When the enemy comes in like a flood, the Spirit of the LORD will lift up a standard against him*" (Isaiah 59:19), we may boldly say, "God's Spirit is raising a standard of defense on my behalf at the very time the enemy is heaping his pressure on me; praise the Lord, my case is His."

Because He has said, "*Our God whom we serve is able to deliver us*" (Daniel 3:17), we may boldly say, "God is my Deliverer in every case because I constantly serve Him."

Because He has said, "*The LORD is near to all who call upon Him, to all who call upon Him in truth*" (Psalm 145:18), we may boldly say, "The Lord is near me now because I call upon Him in truth."

Because He has said, "*The LORD will fight for you, and you shall hold your peace*" (Exodus 14:14), we may boldly say, "I know God is fighting for me because I am holding my peace; I have committed the battle into His hands."

Because He has said, "*Thanks be to God who always leads us in triumph in Christ*" (2 Corinthians 2:14), we may boldly say, "I am more than a conqueror through Christ who loves me." (See Romans 8:37.)

Because He has said, "*No good thing will He withhold from those who walk uprightly*" (Psalm 84:11), we may boldly say, "The Lord is withholding no good thing from me because I am walking uprightly before Him."

Because He has said, "*There is therefore now no condemnation to those who are in Christ Jesus*" (Romans 8:1), we may boldly say, "I have no condemnation because I am in Christ."

Because He has said, "*Casting all your care upon Him, for He cares for you*" (1 Peter 5:7), we may boldly say, "I am free of care because all my cares are cast upon the Lord."

Because He has said, "*The one who comes to Me I will by no means cast out*" (John 6:37), we may boldly say, "I have come with my sins, burdens, and failures, and the Lord has taken me in."

Because He has said, "*Commit your way to the LORD, trust also in Him, and He shall bring it to pass*" (Psalm 37:5), we may boldly say, "The Lord is working out every detail of my life because I have committed of it all to Him, and I am fully trusting Him."

We may boldly say, "Healing is ours."

Because He has said, "*Beloved, I pray that you may prosper in all things and be in health, just as your soul prospers*" (3 John 2), we may boldly say, "I have a right to prosperity and health because I am prospering in my soul."

Because He has said, "*He Himself took our infirmities and bore our sicknesses*" (Matthew 8:17), we may boldly say, "I am free from sicknesses and disease because they were all borne by Jesus Christ for me."

Because He has said, "*He who raised Christ from the dead will also give life to your mortal bodies through His Spirit who dwells in you*" (Romans 8:11), we may boldly say, "God is giving life to my mortal body now by the very same Spirit that raised Jesus from the dead, because His Spirit dwells in me; thus, I am free from weakness and sickness."

Because He has said, "*They will lay hands on the sick, and they will recover*" (Mark 16:18), we may boldly say, when we lay hands on the sick, "They are recovering because I am acting on His Word."

Because He has said, "*You shall serve the* LORD *your God, and He will bless your bread and your water. And I will take sickness away from the midst of you*" (Exodus 23:25), we may boldly say, "Sickness is taken away from me, and my bread and water are blessed because I am serving the Lord my God."

Because He has said, "*To you who fear My name the Sun of Righteousness shall arise with healing in His wings*" (Malachi 4:2), we may boldly say, "The Lord is arising with healing for me now because I fear His name."

Because He has said, "*He sent His word and healed them*" (Psalm 107:20), we may boldly say, "Healing is mine now; the Lord is healing me through His Word because I have received His Word into my life."

We may boldly say, "Our prayers are answered."

Because He has said, "*Before they call, I will answer; and while they are still speaking, I will hear*" (Isaiah 65:24), we may boldly say, "The Lord is answering my prayer even now as I pray. In fact, He was already working on the answer before I prayed."

Because He has said, "*Call to Me, and I will answer you, and show you great and mighty things, which you do not know*" (Jeremiah 33:3), we may boldly say, "The Lord is answering me and showing me great things because I am calling to Him."

Because He has said, "*Whatever you ask in My name, that I will do, that the Father may be glorified in the Son*" (John 14:13), we may boldly say, "The Father is being glorified in the Son because Jesus is doing great things for me as I ask in His name."

Because He has said, "*Delight yourself also in the LORD, and He shall give you the desires of your heart*" (Psalm 37:4), we may boldly say, "The Lord is granting me the desires of my heart because I am delighting myself in Him."

Because He has said, "*If you abide in Me, and My words abide in you, you will ask what you desire, and it shall be done for you*" (John 15:7), we may boldly say, "I am abiding in Christ, He is living in me, and He is answering my petitions."

Because He has said, *"Ask, and you will receive, that your joy may be full"* (John 16:24), we may boldly say, "My joy is full because I am asking and receiving in Jesus' name."

Because He has said, *"Whatever things you ask when you pray, believe that you receive them, and you will have them"* (Mark 11:24), we may boldly say, "I shall have what I have prayed for because I have prayed for it and I believe it is mine even now."

Because He has said, *"Everyone who asks receives"* (Matthew 7:8), we may boldly say, "I know I am receiving because I have asked; 'everyone' means no exceptions, and that includes me."

Negative Confession

Few of us know the power of our own words upon our spirits.

If I confess that I am not feeling well, I don't know whether I will able to stay up all day. My body at once begins to sag. My spirit rises up against that negative confession, but it is conquered, and I go down spiritually and mentally to the level of my confession.

However, if I confess that I can do all things in Christ, He becomes the level of my confession. When I confess that I can do all things in Him, He becomes the strength of my life. Therefore, I confess that I have the ability of God to do the things that He wishes me to do.

He wants me to call on that sick person and open the Scriptures to him. Suppose I have never done such a thing, but I remember the words of Isaiah 53:4–5:

Surely He has borne our griefs and carried our sorrows; yet we esteemed Him stricken, smitten by God, and afflicted. But He was wounded for our transgressions, He was bruised for our iniquities; the chastisement for our peace was upon Him, and by His stripes we are healed.

The Spirit brings that passage home to me. Now, I know that I can explain that Scripture to the sick one. You don't know what joy thrills me! I go to the house, and I greet him as conqueror. I know that the Word is going to work as effectually in him as it has worked effectually in me.

My faith rises to the level of my confession. God's ability in me arises to meet the need of my confession. I have the ability to do anything that He wishes done. He is my strength; He is my sufficiency; He is my fullness; He is all that I need.

Forgetting Certain Words

There are certain words in our vocabularies that should be tabooed, forgotten. They should never be permitted on our lips. If we refuse to speak them, after a bit, the thoughts will die unclothed.

We should stop using the word fear until fear dies out and courage grows big and robust in its place. We have no room for words such as *scandal, hatred, jealousy, bitterness, unbelief,* and *doubt,* or for expressions like "I am a Doubting Thomas."

By using such words, we are telling the great Father God that we have no faith in Him, just like a boy saying to his father, "Father, I have no faith in you. I wish I did have some." It is like a wife saying to her husband, "I have no faith in you."

The above are expressions that ought to die. They ought to be buried without a funeral. We ought to become so ashamed of them that we will never permit them to be spoken in our presence.

There are certain words that are never spoken except in the privacy of our own inner lives. These are words that should never be spoken, even there. Let us call them bad words, dead words. Let us find living words to take their place, loving words, health-giving words, victory words. We find these new words in the Bible.

Wrong Confessions

Just as the right confession of faith will produce positive results in your life, so a wrong confession will produce negative results. The Bible says that "*death and life are in the power of the tongue*" (Proverbs 18:21). Defeat or victory, sickness or health, are in the power of the tongue. Jesus said, "*He will have whatever he says*" (Mark 11:23). Look at these examples of right and wrong confessions.

Wrong Confession: "My sinus condition always gets worse at this time of year."

Right Confession: "I never expect bad experiences any time of the year. I am not a fair-weather Christian. I live boldly by the Word of God. My joy is full because of what the Lord is doing for me. He said, '*Ask, and you will receive, that your joy may be full*' (John 16:24). My joy is full—winter, spring, summer, and fall—because I ask of Him and I receive from Him. The Lord's ability to keep me in good health is not limited to certain seasons, for He '*is the same yesterday, today, and forever*' (Hebrews 13:8). The Lord will do as much for me on one day as He will do for me on another."

Wrong Confession: "I cannot speak in public because I always become very nervous and cannot testify."

Right Confession: "I refuse to give place to fear, for that is giving place to the devil, who is the author of fear. *'God has not given us a spirit of fear, but of power and of love and of a sound mind'* (2 Timothy 1:7). I am absolutely free from all fear, even the fear of speaking in public. God has said, *'Fear not, for I am with you; be not dismayed, for I am your God'* (Isaiah 41:10). I am no longer afraid to testify in public, because God is with me. It is the enemy who would keep me from speaking for my Lord. *'When the enemy comes in like a flood, the Spirit of the LORD will lift up a standard against him'* (Isaiah 59:19). When the enemy heaps his pressure on me, I will praise the Lord that my case is His. He will give me freedom from fear and satanic nervousness. God gives me confidence by saying, *'Go, and I will be with your mouth and teach you what you shall say'* (Exodus 4:12). God is actually with my mouth to guide me in what I say in public for Him. Therefore, I triumph in His ability."

Wrong Confession: "Well, I made it to work today, but that's about all I can say. With the way I feel, I certainly don't expect to get much done."

Right Confession: "I refuse to give place to a gloomy confession that would thoroughly snare my soul. '*You are snared by the words of your mouth*' (Proverbs 6:2). I serve God continually, so I am assured of deliverance from such a pessimistic attitude that would crush my spirit and defeat my soul. '*Your God, whom you serve continually, He will deliver you*' (Daniel 6:16). God is my Deliverer in every situation, for I serve Him constantly. '*Thanks be to God who always leads us in triumph in Christ*' (2 Corinthians 2:14). On my job, in my home, in my service for the Lord—in whatever I do—I am more than a conqueror through Christ who loves me. (See Romans 8:37.) I reject the attitude that leaves me barely able to keep my head above water. God is showing me great and mighty things in life, for He has promised, '*Call to Me, and I will answer you, and show you great and mighty things, which you do not know*' (Jeremiah 33:3). I call to Him; He is answering me and is showing me great and mighty things."

Wrong Confession: "I failed to get that promotion I had hoped for, but it's just as I expected—I never seem to succeed at anything."

Right Confession: "I do not believe that adverse forces are overthrowing God's work on my behalf. The Lord is working on the answers even before I pray: '*Before they call, I will answer; and while they are still speaking, I will hear*' (Isaiah 65:24). I do not expect failure. I expect success. Jesus didn't come to give me a lackluster life. He said, '*I have come that they may have life, and that they may have it more abundantly*' (John 10:10). Because I have received Jesus Christ as my Savior and Lord, I have that abundant life in me now. I know God is prospering my life: '*Beloved, I pray that you may prosper in all things and be in health, just as your soul prospers*' (3 John 2). I have a right to prosperity and health, and I am prospering in my soul. God has promised to bless me richly because I am a giver: '*Give, and it will be given to you: good measure, pressed down, shaken together, and running over will be put into your bosom*' (Luke 6:38). Yes, the Lord is heaping up my blessings, for I am giving to Him and His work. I am blessed."

Wrong Confession: "I don't feel very well. I believe I'm getting the flu."

Right Confession: "Praise the Lord, I don't live by my feelings, for they change like the weather. I live by faith, which is living by the Word of God. Why should I get the flu when Jesus Himself took my infirmities and bore my sicknesses? (See Matthew 8:17.) I am not going to take anything bad, because Jesus took it all for me. I will resist taking anything the devil would put upon me. I will live in the victory of Jesus' substitutionary sacrifice. He is my sin-substitute and my sickness-substitute. I praise His name for what He has worked for me."

Wrong Confession: "I wonder if I will ever feel any better."

Right Confession: "Regardless of my present condition, I know the Lord will restore health to me, for this is His promise in Jeremiah 30:17: '*I will restore health to you.*' I don't worry about it. God watches over His Word to perform it (see Jeremiah 1:12), and "*God is not a man, that He should lie*" (Numbers 23:19). I know I will feel better, not because of hopes or wishes, but because of His Word to me. '*He sent His word and healed them*' (Psalm 107:20). I have received His healing Word, and I praise Him that His Word is sure. Jesus said that according to my expectations, or my faith, it shall be to me. (See Matthew 9:29.) I fully expect to feel better because His Word is prevailing in my life."

Wrong Confession: "I don't know what I will do financially. The cost of living keeps going up."

Right Confession: "I live by the sure Word of God: '*My God shall supply all your need according to His riches in glory by Christ Jesus*' (Philippians 4:19). Regardless of inflation, my God shall minister to all my needs. I do not walk in the counsel of the ungodly, stand in the path of sinners, or sit in the seat of the scornful. I delight myself in the Word of God; both day and night, I meditate on it. I am like a tree planted by the waters; I am bearing fruit. As a result, whatever I do shall prosper. (See Psalm 1:1–3.) If the cost of living keeps going up, God's prosperity in my life shall increase. I do not fear inflation. The Lord is my Supply."

Wrong Confession: "I just knew it would rain today. It always rains when we plan anything outdoors."

Right Confession: "I will not be ruled by a pessimistic attitude. I live with expectation of success. Whatever the weather may be, I will confess, '*This is the day the LORD has made; we will rejoice and be glad in it*' (Psalm 118:24)."

Wrong Confession: "Why does this always have to happen to me?"

Right Confession: "I expect nothing evil or bad to happen to me. I live by God's Word, which promises, '*No evil shall befall you, nor shall any plague come near your dwelling*' (Psalm 91:10). God commands me to commit my way to Him and trust in Him, and '*He shall bring it to pass*' (Psalm 37:5). I expect Him to bring about good things, not bad ones. As a sincere Christian, I seek to walk uprightly before Him. He assures me, '*No good thing will He withhold from those who walk uprightly*' (Psalm 84:11). Something good will always happen to me!"

Wrong Confession: "I will try to come if things work out, but the prospect isn't too promising."

Right Confession: "I face life and its challenges with a positive confession, a bold confession. I am waiting on the Lord, and He is renewing my strength. (See Isaiah 40:31.) I am keeping my mind stayed upon the Lord, and He is keeping me in perfect peace. (See Isaiah 26:3.) I fully expect things to work out, for I delight myself in the Lord, and He gives me the desires of my heart. (See Psalm 37:4.) Jesus said, '*Go your way; and as you have believed, so let it be done for you*' (Matthew 8:13), and I believe that right things work out for me. I will keep my appointments, because I believe that way. I reject negative confessions of doubt, fear, and uncertainty. The Lord is giving me victory in all situations. '*The LORD will fight for you, and you shall hold your peace*' (Exodus 14:14)."

Wrong Confession: "I won't dare to attempt this particular task, as it is beyond my ability."

Right Confession: "My ability is measured by God's ability. '*If God is for us, who can be against us?*' (Romans 8:31). God is for me, so I can do all things through Him who is my strength and sufficiency. (See Philippians 4:13.) I never minimize my ability, for I know the truth, and truth sets me free. (See John 8:32.) I am made strong with His strength: '*Let the weak say, "I am strong"*' (Joel 3:10). I say boldly in the face of supposed weakness, 'I am strong; I count on the mighty One who gives life to my mortal body. "*He who raised Christ from the dead will also give life to your mortal bodies through His Spirit who dwells in you*" (Romans 8:11). God gives life to my mortal body now by the very same Spirit that raised Jesus from the dead, because His Spirit dwells in me. Thus, I can face any task and succeed because of His unlimited ability within me.'"

Wrong Confession: "I will probably be unable to do that, as I doubt that I will have the money in time."

Right Confession: "I will not defeat myself by forecasting failure. I don't entertain pessimism about any of my life's plans. Jesus has given me some great assurances about life. He declared, *'For everyone who asks receives'* (Matthew 7:8). That includes me. I know that I am receiving those good and necessary things from the Lord, because I have asked Him. I am receiving, for His promise contains no exceptions. I am free of care about the future, for I have joyfully cast all of my cares upon the One who really cares for me. (See 1 Peter 5:7.) I am sure that God will supply all of the money I need in plenty of time to meet my needs."

Wrong Confession: "I think I am catching my husband's cold."

Right Confession: "Why should I catch anyone's cold? I do not fear a cold because I fear the name of the Lord. *'To you who fear My name the Sun of Righteousness shall arise with healing in His wings'* (Malachi 4:2). I am not bound by the traditional thinking that says a sickness must run its course in a family. I am serving Jesus, and He has assured me, *'You shall serve the Lord your God, and He will bless your bread and your water. And I will take sickness away from the midst of you'* (Exodus 23:25). Sickness is taken away from me and my family because we serve the Lord."

Believing

G od so loved the world that He gave His only begotten Son, that whoever believes in Him should not perish but have everlasting life" (John 3:16). The Father gave Jesus to the world, to the perishing ones.

He gave Jesus to the men who crucified Him. He gave Jesus to the men who made a crown of thorns and pressed it upon the brow of His Son. He gave Jesus to the men who nailed Him to the cross. He gave Jesus to Pilate and to the cruel, wicked, selfish Caiphas, the high priest. Strange, isn't it?

That act brings us face-to-face with a strange word. You don't find it being used this way in the Old Testament, and it is used in regard to Jesus only a few times. The word is *grace*. "*The law was given through Moses, but grace and truth came through Jesus Christ*" (John 1:17).

What is grace? It is love at work; love giving; love doing for the unlovely and unworthy. The gift of Jesus was love's spontaneous outburst. God calls it grace.

Now, what does it mean to believe in Jesus? We all know that the word *believe* is a verb. We know that *faith* is a noun. Believing is an action word; faith is the result of a person's having acted or believed. Believing in the New Testament sense, in the sense of the Pauline revelation, means possession—action that ends with possession.

Jesus gave us the key in John 6:47: "*He who believes in Me has everlasting life.*" In the mind of the Father, believing is possession, and to gain possession, we act on His Word. Believing, then, is acting on what the Father has spoken.

When I believe in Christ, that means I have taken possession of what the Father has given me. Jesus is mine. He is my Savior, He is my Lord, and He is my Life! The moment we take possession of Christ, we become new creations. We are "*born from above*" (John 3:3 NRSV).

You see, believing is an act of the will. It is a choice. It is a decision. It means that I am willing to turn my back on my past life and have it wiped out, have it remitted, and have it stop being. I am ready to begin a new life now without any past—to step out into a new realm. I am ready to be translated out of the realm of death, darkness, and sin, into the realm of life and love, where I will become a child of God.

Believing means that I am ready to take possession of what God in His great love gave me. He gave me Christ. He made me a present of eternal life. He gave me all that Christ was, all that He did, and all that He is today.

I accept that truth, I take possession of the gift, and I look up and say, "Father, I thank You for Jesus and for the gift of eternal life that comes with Jesus. I thank You for the remission of all my sins, the wiping out of my past. I thank You that I am now a new creation. I thank You, Father, that Ephesians 1:3 has become a reality: *'Blessed be the God and Father of our Lord Jesus Christ, who has blessed us with every spiritual blessing in the heavenly places in Christ.'*"

God chose me in Christ before the foundation of the world (see verse 4), and now I have responded to that call and have become His. I am now coming into my inheritance.

All these years, rest and peace of heart belonged to me, but I did not know it. The name of Jesus, with all its power and its rights, has been mine, but I never took possession of it. I have a vast inheritance in Christ, but I chose to live in poverty within sight of my inheritance and riches.

Now I am taking possession. I have lived in weakness when strength belonged to me. I have lived in helplessness when the ability of God was mine. I have lived in ignorance when the wisdom and knowledge of the Son of God were all mine. They belonged to me—they had been given to me—but I ignored the gift and never thanked the Giver. At last, my eyes are open. I see my rights, and I take them.

You see, believing is taking possession. It is simply acting on the Word of the Father. It's a beautiful thing, isn't it? It's so simple.

I tell the world what I am in Christ. I tell the world that Christ is my Lord and Savior. I shout aloud that there is now no condemnation for me, for I am in Christ Jesus.

The possession did not come until I made my joyful confession. When I made that, all became mine in reality.

There is no possession without confession. Realization follows confession. I begin to act on the Word, and the possession becomes a real thing to me. I then "cash in" on what grace has given me. It was never a problem of faith or emotion—it was a problem of my not taking what God had already given me.

Great Confessions

The word *confession* in the Bible means affirming what God has said in His Word. It is witnessing to the Word's declaration. It is testifying to truths revealed in the Bible.

Affirmations of Truth

We have been divinely instructed to "*hold fast our confession*" (Hebrews 4:14). The writer of the book of Hebrews further stated, "*Let us hold fast the confession of our hope without wavering, for He who promised is faithful*" (Hebrews 10:23). Not only are we to hold fast our confession of the Word, but we are also to affirm constantly those things that God has revealed to us. (See Titus 3:8.)

Confession is saying what God has said in His Word about a certain thing. It is agreeing with God. It is saying the same thing that Scripture says. To hold fast your confession is to say, over and over, what God has said until the thing desired in your heart and promised in the Word is fully manifested. There is no such thing as possession without confession.

When we discover our rights in Christ, we are to affirm those things constantly. Testify to them. Witness those tremendous Bible facts. The apostle Paul said, "*The sharing of your faith may become effective by the acknowledgment of every good thing which is in you in Christ Jesus*" (Philemon 6).

Affirmations of truth should ring from our lips constantly. We are to hold fast to them without wavering. The penalty for wavering in our confession is that we deny ourselves God's promise and the performance of it. "*Let him ask in faith, with no doubting, for he who doubts is like a wave of the sea driven and tossed by the wind. For let not that man suppose that he will receive anything from the Lord*" (James 1:6–7).

The psalmist said, "*Let the redeemed of the Lord say so*" (Psalm 107:2), and again, "*Let those who love Your salvation say continually, 'Let God be magnified!'*" (Psalm 70:4). What things are we to affirm constantly? Affirm the Scriptures that reveal the good things within us in Christ.

There are hundreds of powerful affirmations to make constantly as we speak the language of Scripture. For example, some things that we are to affirm constantly are:

- God is who He says He is.
- I am who God says I am.
- God can do what He says He can do.
- I can do what God says I can do.
- God has what He says He has.
- I have what God says I have.

We know that in Jesus Christ we have been given salvation, not just for our souls, but also for our bodies in our health, our finances, our peace of mind, and our freedom from bondage and fear.

Words That Work Wonders

If only we would realize the power in our words, how different our lives would be. It has been said that "the pen is mightier than the sword." How much mightier the words of our pens and of our mouths when our words are the Word of God! *"Whoever offers praise glorifies Me; and to him who orders his conduct aright I will show the salvation of God"* (Psalm 50:23). Some words that can work wonders are...

Words of Praise. *"I will bless the LORD at all times; His praise shall continually be in my mouth"* (Psalm 34:1). Resolve to be a bold "praiser" from now on. As a praiser, extol the Lord, not so much for the gifts you've received, but magnify the wonderful Giver Himself.

Words of Edification and Grace. Resolve to order your conversation aright, so that *"no corrupt word proceed out of your mouth, but what is good for necessary edification, that it may impart grace to the hearers*" (Ephesians 4:29).

Words of Bold Authority That Overcome Satan's Power. "*They overcame him by the blood of the Lamb and by the word of their testimony*" (Revelation 12:11).

Words of Confession of God's Word. Confession always precedes possession. The word *confess* means "to say the same thing." Dare to say exactly what God says in His Word. Agree with God by speaking His Word in all circumstances.

When we order our words aright, God manifests the benefits of His great salvation. "*With the mouth confession is made unto salvation*" (Romans 10:10). And remember that when we make confession unto salvation, it includes healing, deliverance, and every spiritual and physical blessing provided for us in Christ's atonement.

As confession always precedes possession, so a wrong confession, a negative confession, precedes the possession of wrong things. Your tongue, used wrongly, can cause you much trouble. "*Whoever guards his mouth and tongue keeps his soul from troubles*" (Proverbs 21:23). "*You are snared by the words of your mouth; you are taken by the words of your mouth*" (Proverbs 6:2). Refuse to give a wrong confession.

Remember that your words can work wonders. Therefore, speak words of praise, words of singing, words of faith in God's Word, and words of bold

46

authority, expelling Satan's power. Truly, words are the coin of the kingdom, and you can boldly speak words that will work wonders for you!

The Value of Testifying

The nation of Israel was God's testimony while the Israelites lived in Palestine. All the land traffic between Babylon, Damascus, and Egypt had to pass through Palestine. The Israelites were God's ancient witnesses. It was a sad day when they lost that witness and were carried into captivity.

We are God's testimony today. "*You shall be witnesses to Me*" (Acts 1:8) means that we are each a testimony. It is significant that our faith never rises above our testimonies.

If you are afraid to testify out loud, faith dies or becomes feeble and helpless. Your testimony is your faith expressed. "*If you confess with your mouth the Lord Jesus...*" (Romans 10:9). It is a lip confession. If you confess before the world and maintain your confession, never giving it up, never yielding to a second confession, you are expressing faith.

A second confession can contradict the first. When the writer of Hebrews told us to hold fast to our confession, he was striking at the very root of Christianity. (See Hebrews 10:23.) You will never grow beyond your confession. *"They overcame him by the blood of the Lamb and by the word of their testimony"* (Revelation 12:11).

Sin-consciousness has its own confession, just as righteousness-consciousness has its confession. Satan is the inspirer of the testimony of sin-consciousness, just as the Holy Spirit is the inspiration for the testimony of righteousness.

Every testimony of weakness and failure glorifies the one who makes you weak. It is Satan's testimony through your lips. When you confess that your prayers are not answered, you are charging God with falsehood, and you are lending your lips to the devil to give his testimony of his supremacy over God.

When you say, "I have been prayed for again and again and have not received my healing," you are glorifying the adversary. It is your testimony of lack, unbelief, and failure that has held you in bondage.

If you give a testimony of faith and maintain it in the presence of every provocation, believing that God's Word is true and that *"by His stripes we are healed"* (Isaiah 53:5), you will be healed.

Your lack of money, your lack of strength, and your lack of usefulness in the cause of Christ are the products of your own testimony.

Some people have two testimonies. One is for public consumption and the other is a private testimony. Their private testimonies are failure and lack. Their public testimonies are feeble, weakened, and almost cringing, barely able to say that God's Word is true.

It is that frank, absolute testimony of the victories in Christ that gives birth to faith in other people's hearts. Have but one testimony—that of the absolute faithfulness of God and of your absolute confidence in His Word.

Bold Faith

Boldness

Beloved, if our heart does not condemn us, we have confidence toward God. (1 John 3:21)

The secret of victory is grasping your dilemma with both hands. The secret of winning is to face the difficulty with a consciousness that it cannot whip you, because it cannot whip God. The way to face an impossible situation is to realize that you are linked up with God; and he who is linked with God can no more fail than God can fail.

The faith that Jesus had in Himself, in His ministry, and in His Father made Him face the cross with the spirit of a conqueror. When one is linked with God, the resources of God are his. God underwrites every enterprise into which He sends you.

You may not feel the thrill and emotion that you would think natural when one is linked up with omnipotence. But you do not need to feel it. All you need is to know that greater is He who is in you, who is energizing you, than all the opposition that could possibly come. (See 1 John 4:4.) With a holy calmness, you can face life's problems and life's difficulties.

A Settled Conviction

Boldness is not arrogance, bravado, or pretense. It is courage; it is confidence; it is faith in God. It is this settled conviction that greater is He who strengthens your arm and who guides your work than any force that either humans or demons can bring against you. Boldness is that silent assurance that with God, you must prevail.

The roots of your being go down into the very heart and bosom of God. For you to be uprooted would be to uproot the very heart of God. Our boldness is born of a conscious union with God in doing His will, in achieving His desire, and in carrying forward His program.

All the faculties of your being have been lined up with God. It is His wisdom that you depend on. It is His grace that you drink deeply. It is His power that strengthens you in the struggle. Faith has enabled you to face life's problems with a smile.

Faith in Him, the unseen One, has lifted you out of your weakness and into His sphere. You live and walk in the strength of God. You are in the midst of His enduring strength. You draw your life from Him. His life is your life. You are hidden with Christ in God. (See Colossians 3:3.)

Come Boldly to the Throne of Grace

The words of Jesus allow us to know Him. Silent pictures of Jesus could not convey to us the true Jesus, so we have speaking pictures of Jesus. We see Him acting the part. We hear His words.

The words are the things that live longest in our minds. His Word is Himself. That is a startling thing when you think about it. When He says, "*Come boldly to the throne of grace*" to make your requests known (Hebrews 4:16), we come with lips filled with His Word. We come in the name of Jesus.

We come on the authority of His own promise, where He said, "*Whatever you ask the Father in My name He will give you*" (John 16:23). That word is His Word. That makes Him utter the prayer that our lips are saying. "*If two of you agree on earth concerning anything that they ask, it will be done for them by My Father in heaven*" (Matthew 18:19). When I quote His Word, His Word goes up before the Father. It is His Word. It is not mine. It is His prayer, not my prayer.

Jesus said, "*If you abide in Me, and My words abide in you, you will ask what you desire, and it shall be done for you*" (John 15:7). I am using Jesus' words. The Father hears the words of Jesus coming from lips yielded to the lordship of His Son, so it is really His Son praying through these lips. I remind Him that the Word does abide in me, and I

54

do abide in Him. There is no ignoring it. It is the Master Himself doing the work.

He prays through me. I quote John 14:13 before the Father: "*Whatever you ask in My name, that I will do, that the Father may be glorified in the Son.*" I say to the Father, "I desire that You will be glorified through Jesus, so I am asking in Jesus' name that this thing be done."

The word *ask* can mean "demand." I am demanding that the soreness leave this person's body. I know that when this takes place, the Father is being glorified. I am taking Jesus' side of the issue, and I am doing the thing that will glorify the Father.

When we take this attitude, prayer becomes a God-sized affair. We are entering into the fullness of Christ in the prayer life. Sitting in our homes, or wherever we are, we can touch the utmost islands of the sea. We can send angel forces to minister to those in need.

His Word becomes the coin of the kingdom. His name on our lips becomes as though the Master Himself were present. Let us enter into this powerful relationship in all its fullness.

The Power of the Bloodline

What do you do when you are in desperate situations? For example, is there any solution for dealing with break-ins and thefts?

Yes, there is a power in the blood of Jesus that will overcome anything and everything the enemy may bring against us. Revelation 12:11 became alive to me, my family, and our ministry in overcoming deep adversity. It says, *"They overcame him by the blood of the Lamb and by the word of their testimony."*

For more than forty years, we have lived in a fresh way under the protection of applying this verse. We have lived free from the peril of being victimized by a wicked, unfeeling devil and his designated work: *"The thief does not come except to steal, and to kill, and to destroy"* (John 10:10).

In 1969, our evangelistic offices in Surrey, Canada, were under siege by the enemy. Repeatedly, thieves broke into our offices during the night to steal and to devastate the premises. We used every natural means to put a stop to the onslaughts, including increased lights, locks, security, and police surveillance, but nothing availed; the attacks persisted.

There were nights when I would wake up in a cold sweat with a premonition that our offices were being broken into at that very moment. I would jump into my clothes and drive to our offices. More than once, I discovered that as the headlights of my car would strike the front of the large building, the thieves would escape out the back door. It was frustrating and disturbing.

Then, an evangelist named Stevens came to Canada for ministry. The Lord used him to win souls to Christ and to break strongholds over the lives of people. The devil became infuriated and told Brother Stevens, "I am going to kill your children on your farm down in Tennessee."

Brother Stevens laughed at the devil and responded, "Satan, you can't touch my children. They belong to Jesus!"

But Satan countered, "I have put rabies in the foxes that roam the woods next to your farm. They will come across your boundary line to bite your children and infect them with rabies. They will die."

Brother Stevens was experienced in dealing with the devil. He knew that this threat by the adversary was not a call for him to go buy an airplane ticket, fly back to Tennessee, and go hunting for foxes with his shotgun. Rather, he discerned that it was a spiritual attack, and he was fully aware of the power of the blood, as taught in Exodus 12:23: "*When He sees the blood on the lintel and on the two doorposts, the LORD will pass over the door and not allow the destroyer to come into your houses.*"

He asked three believers to join with him in applying Revelation 12:11 in this situation: "*They overcame him by the blood of the Lamb and by the word of their testimony.*" They each held up an index finger and, by faith, drew a bloodline around his farm, specifically around the boundary lines.

Within ten days, Brother Stevens received a letter from his brother, who was caring for the farm. He wrote, "I was walking on the backside of your land, I came to your boundary line, and I found five foxes lying dead on the ground. I had their heads examined, and all five of them were filled with rabies."

Thank God those foxes could not cross that boundary line! In the realm of the Spirit, that was the bloodline. The blood of Jesus had been applied by "*the word of their testimony,*" and the foxes had all dropped dead.

When I heard that story, I knew that this was the answer for our offices. I called my family and staff together. We each held up an index finger and, by faith, drew a bloodline around our offices. We knew that the authority was in the blood and the words that came out of our mouths. The moving of our fingers was symbolic of our affirmation.

We declared, "Devil, you have done your evil work against us. Now, we apply the blood of Jesus against you. No longer can you cause evil men to break into our offices. The blood of Jesus is against you, and we overcome you!"

By the power of the blood of Jesus, those intruders never broke into our offices again. If they tried, they were forbidden from crossing the boundary line. There is power—wonder-working power—in the blood of the Lamb! All the measures we had tried before this had failed. Putting in new lights and installing new locks did not stop the thieves. Increased police surveillance did not apprehend the thieves. It was only the power of the precious blood of Jesus, as spoken through our affirmation in an act of faith, that stopped the thieves.

In all the decades that have passed since that time, we have never had another break-in. We have enlarged this faith action to include not only our offices, but also our homes, our cars, our furniture, our clothing, our possessions, and our mission trips. Most of all, we have applied the power and the protection of the blood over our family members.

My wife and I often travel more than 100,000 miles each year in doing the Lord's work and taking the gospel to the nations. Whenever we board a flight, we fasten our seat belts and immediately draw a bloodline around the big jet, the engines, the flight crew, and our luggage. We are persuaded that we are the safest people in the world, protected by the blood of Jesus.

I challenge you to take this action: hold up your index finger and make a circle as you cover your life, your vehicle, your home, and your loved ones with the precious blood of Jesus. For over forty years, God has wonderfully honored our faith in the blood of Jesus.

We are not among those whom Satan conquers with his foul works. Rather, we overcome him by the blood of the Lamb and the word of our testimony. What a life of confidence this faith action brings!

Our Solid Front in Christ

Our solid front in Christ" means a fearless confession in the presence of circumstances that seem overwhelming.

Your fearlessness will be a token of impending destruction to your enemies, but to you it will be a sure token of your salvation from God. (See Philippians 1:28.) A fearless stand in the presence of defeat brings victory. A fearless confession of the supremacy of God over all oppression of disease brings victory.

God cannot lie, and His Word can never fail. He says, "*I am ready to perform My word*" (Jeremiah 1:12). We need nothing more than that. Romans 10:11 is God's very message to our hearts: "*Whoever believes on Him will not be put to shame.*" You see, God and His Word are one, so you dare to fearlessly take your place as one of His own with Christ.

"*Though I am absent in the flesh, yet I am with you in spirit, rejoicing to see your good order and the steadfastness of your faith in Christ*" (Colossians 2:5). The Weymouth translation says, "*...the solid front presented by your faith in Christ.*" Another translation puts it, "*...your steadiness and solid front in Christ.*"

The wavering, halting, doubting testimony breeds inability and failure, but the one who dares to face the adversary fearlessly is the winner. This means daring in the face of every problem to hold fast to your confession. (See Hebrews 4:14.) It is not *your* profession—it is your confession of who He is to you and what *His Word* means to you in your daily walk.

We know the Word, and it is necessary that we act upon it so that we become doers of the Word and practicers of the Word. (See James 1:22–25.) Our confession and our conduct must agree. You are familiar with this passage from the book of James:

> *What does it profit, my brethren, if someone says he has faith but does not have works? Can faith save him?...But someone will say, "You have faith, and I have works." Show me your faith without your works, and I will show you my faith by my works.* (James 2:14, 18)

The mere mental assenter has no corresponding actions; the one who "hopes" has no corresponding actions. It is the one who believes who acts upon the Word, brings glory to the Father, and brings joy to Jesus.

You see, in every place, there must be a corresponding action. We must never for one moment forget what manner of people we are. We are the "new creation" people. We are a people indwelt by God. We are an overcoming people. We must remember what we are in Christ. "*In all these things we are more than conquerors*" (Romans 8:37). We are masters of circumstances.

The man who is independent of circumstances will tell you that in poverty, he acts as though he were rich; in prison, he plays the part of a free man. Circumstances cannot rule him. Demons have learned to fear him. God honors him. Jesus rejoices in him. He is a master. If sickness overtakes him, he remembers that he is a master of sickness and praises the Father for his perfect healing. If financial difficulties arise, he remembers, "*Your heavenly Father knows that you need all these things. But seek first the kingdom of God and His righteousness, and all these things shall be added to you*" (Matthew 6:32–33).

Such a man has sought the kingdom, and he has found it. He has found his place as a son of God; consequently, he is a master over need. He cultivates the "God inside" consciousness. Your walk with God can be masterful if you will cultivate the consciousness of your oneness with Christ, of your victory in Him over the forces of darkness. Cultivate a consciousness of the utter mastery of Jesus' name. Remember that He said, "*In My name they will cast out demons*" (Mark 16:17), and, "*Whatever you ask the Father in My name He will give you*" (John 16:23).

If you have access to the Father in that name, it puts you in the winning for eternity. You are a master now. Remember what manner of man you are, and do not go back and live as a common man. Live as the Master did in His earthly walk, because you have God in you. You have the legal right to use His name, which has all authority. You are a master. Praise Him for it, and go live it now.

How Faith Is Built

"Faith is the substance of things hoped for" (Hebrews 11:1). We give substance to hope when we act on the Word. Hope is always future. Faith is now. Believing is acting on the Word.

James said, "Be doers of the word, and not hearers only, deceiving yourselves" (James 1:22). A "doer" is a "liver." The Word lives in me to the measure that I do it. Doing the Word, then, is living the Word. This means that God is actually living in me. I live in the Word to the measure that it functions in my daily life.

Jesus said, "If you abide in Me, and My words abide in you…" (John 15:7). With this reality, prayer becomes so simple. Why? Because the Word on my lips will be God's Word. God is speaking back to Himself through my lips. Through my lips, God can ask what He will, and it will be given to me.

His Word becomes a living thing on my lips, just as it was a living thing on Jesus' lips. At Lazarus' tomb, Jesus said, "Father, I thank You that You have *heard Me. And I know that You always hear Me"* (John 11:41–42). When the Word abides in you as it lives in Jesus, you can say the same thing to the Father. That Word can abide in us, can live in us, as it lived in Jesus.

When we took Christ, we received eternal life. That brought us into God's family, where we are to assume the place of sons and daughters. Now, we are to act as though we are children of God. We are to take our place and assume our responsibilities.

You are not *trying* to be a child of God. You *are* one. You are not trying to get faith, because all things belong to you since you are in His family. You are doing your Father's will as Jesus did, and the Father is backing you up as He backed up Jesus.

You study to become acquainted with the Father. *"That they may know You, the only true God, and Jesus Christ whom You have sent"* (John 17:3). Did you notice what you just read? That you may know the Father. That you may know Jesus. That you may get acquainted with your Father, knowing Him through Jesus.

You may know Him through the four Gospels, to a degree. You may get to know Him more fully in the Pauline revelation. But you really get to know Him when you begin to practice the Word.

When you become a "doer" of the Word, then you really get to know Him. When you pray with those who are sick; when you learn to discredit sensory evidence that would contradict the Word; when you study the Word as though it were the Father's present message to you; then, you will know Him.

Talk with Him. Fellowship with Him as you would with a loved one living with you. Then you will know the Father.

Results from Prayer

There should be schools to teach men to pray. Prayer is more important than preaching. I mean that kind of prayer that interests God in our welfare—the kind that brings divine response and bona fide answers.

We have plenty of people who pray, but the results do not prove that their prayers were of any value. We must pray to profit. Great businessmen seek to do business to profit. Great steel industries demand the best scientific and technical education, and the same is true in every department of industry.

Prayer is of first importance. Simply talking off into the air is not prayer. Taking up twenty minutes on Sunday morning, giving God a homily on what His duties are toward the nation, is not prayer. Giving the congregation a lecture over God's shoulder is not prayer.

I believe that we should pray for results. If we pray and nothing follows, we should seek what is the trouble. The big things of Christianity are all supernatural, and if things are not done, it shows that we have the form without the power. (See 2 Timothy 3:5.) All things are offered to us through prayer, and if we do not have them, it is because we have not made our prayer connection.

We know that God has heard prayer. You know it, and I know it. I have seen thousands of souls saved in answer to prayer. I have seen thousands of dollars come in answer to prayer. I have seen demons cast out and thousands healed of diseases in answer to prayer. I have seen the miraculous power of God manifested hundreds and thousands of times.

I have gone from church to church and found from twenty to one hundred Christians in almost every place. In many of them, not a soul has been saved for years, and not a striking answer to prayer has been obtained, and yet they keep on praying.

No results! Why not get down to first principles and find out what is the matter? Is God untrue? Is the day of praying over? Have these promises been made by a bankrupt God? It may be that we are not known in the bank of heaven. We had better get Jesus to introduce us and identify us there!

Jesus has given us the right of attorney to use His name in prayer to the Father. His words are final: "*Whatever you ask the Father in My name He will give you*" (John 16:23). We know that Jesus and the Father entered into a wonderful blood covenant with us, and this alone guarantees us answers to our prayers.

Then, Jesus gave us the Great Commission and said that He would be with us until the end of the age. (See Matthew 28:18–20.) If He sends us out, He will back us up, for no soldier goes out under his own orders. Jesus must answer our prayers and meet our needs.

We are faced with great needs everywhere. Men are dying for need of Christ. The sick need healing and the weak need strength. Are you in His will? Are you doing what He wants you to do? Is your life right with God? Does your heart condemn you? If so, get right! Get down before the mighty One and believe your way through the hosts of demons who would hinder your prayers.

Pray to victory. If you are praying for the sick, stick to it and don't give up. If you are praying for money, command it to be loosened in the mighty name of Jesus. If you are praying for souls, stand by until you see the answer.

Bold as a Lion

When I was a young man, I experienced tormenting fears in many areas of my life. I was reluctant, hesitant, and fearful. Then, the Lord called me into the ministry, and He miraculously transformed me from that fearful young man into an excited servant of God. For many years, I lived free from fear in all of its forms. Then, I experienced a crisis that once again brought me face-to-face with the difference between fearful, defeated living and the victory of bold Bible living.

For years, there had been a mole on the side of my face. It was flat, about the size of my fingernail. When the mole began to change in color and size, it became ugly in appearance. In February 1976, my wife, Joyce, and I were preparing to leave for an overseas mission. We were having breakfast with our children when my son spoke up for all of them: "Dad, we're worried about that growth on the side of your head. Before you leave for this trip, we wish you would go to the doctor for an examination."

I consented to my children's request, and, that same afternoon, I went to a doctor's office. The doctor carefully examined the growth and then asked me, in a serious tone of voice, "Reverend Gossett, how soon can you be ready for surgery?"

"Surgery?" I inquired. "I had no idea that you had such an action in mind."

The doctor responded, "It is imperative that you have surgery done as soon as possible. We must not delay." I informed the doctor that we would be away until March 1. He looked at his calendar and then scheduled my surgery for March 4. He gravely informed me of the potential danger of the growth and that the surgery must not be postponed any later than that date.

When Joyce and I arrived overseas a few days later, I was battling with intense fears about the doctor's verdict. In fact, I was having a pity party. *Why should this happen to me? Why should I be the "victim" of such a threatening situation?*

One day, I was standing and looking at myself in the mirror, lightly touching the growth and remembering the doctor's warning of its potential danger. Joyce saw me standing there and spoke out, "Somebody I know is having some real fears."

"Yes, that's right, honey," I admitted.

Joyce walked across the room to me, and I thought she was coming to share some words of tender, loving care. But when she was just a few feet from me, she looked at me sharply and said, "Shame on you!"

"Shame on me? Why did you say that?" I asked.

"You are the preacher who has written books on how to overcome fear; you have shared dozens of radio messages around the world on living free from fear all the days of your life. And now, here you are fearing."

"But, honey, this is for real…."

My wife boldly took action. She said to me, "Don, there are three things we must remember. First, surgery may be God's way of providing for you in this situation. Second, surgery may not be necessary, because the Lord may heal you in His own sovereignty. Third, whatever happens, we must not give place to fear, because that would be giving place to the devil."

With those words, Joyce staunchly placed her hand upon my chest and began to rebuke the spirit of fear in the name of Jesus. That was one of the most remarkable liberations of my life! Suddenly, the fear was all gone. It was as if a fetter had broken from my chest. I was free to breathe deeply without any fear in my heart.

The growth persisted and even became larger and uglier in the days ahead, but I never feared it again. The Lord had liberated me totally from the tormenting spirits of fear, and I was free to praise God, confess His Word, and boldly anticipate the Lord's miracle for my life.

When we were flying home on March 1, I reached up and accidentally touched the growth. When I did so, about one half of it fell off into my hand. Then, during the night of March 3, a tremendous miracle occurred. I rose early the next morning, felt my head, and was delighted to discover that where the rest of the growth had been, there was nothing there! I rushed to the mirror to examine it more closely and found that the growth was completely gone. Returning to my bed, I saw the remains of that growth scattered in the bedsheets.

Joyfully, I awakened Joyce and shared the wonderful news. "Honey, this is the day I'm scheduled for surgery, and there's nothing to 'surge'!" We rejoiced together at what the Lord had done.

At breakfast, we decided that I should keep the appointment for the scheduled surgery. I asked, a little curiously, "What am I going to say to the doctors today? Nothing like this has ever happened to me before."

My son declared in a strong voice, "Dad, when you meet with those doctors today, just tell it like it is!"

When I arrived at the clinic for the scheduled surgery, I was met by a nurse. She led me to the room where I was to leave my clothes and wait until they were ready to perform the surgery. Just as we reached the room, I said, "Nurse, you may not have noticed, but I don't have the growth anymore."

She looked astonished. "You don't have the growth? What happened to it?"

With joy in my heart, I replied, "The Lord Jesus Christ has healed it completely!"

At the mention of the Lord healing me, the nurse looked rather frightened and quickly said, "I must get the doctors immediately." She scurried down the hall, away from the room.

In a few moments, the first doctor returned with my medical chart in his hand. He studied the chart and then carefully examined my head. He repeated this process several times and then explained, "I better get the other doctor. He was involved in your case more than I was."

After a while, the second doctor arrived. The doctor was somewhat dubious about my account that the Lord had worked a miracle for me. He eyed me curiously and asked, "What's this I hear about you working a wonder on yourself?"

"Doctor, I didn't do it. The Lord has done it, and I give Him the thanks and glory!"

For the next twenty minutes, these physicians discussed the entire matter with me. I shared my experience exactly as it had happened: how I had almost succumbed to the spirit of fear, how Joyce had prayed for me, and how the Lord had begun the healing process in the seventy-two hours before the scheduled surgery. As I spoke, the doctors seemed to relax and were much more open in their attitudes.

After some time, the first doctor turned to the second one and asked, "Could this have been a work of nature?" But the other doctor only replied, "What is nature?" As our discussion came to a close, both doctors pronounced my case dismissed. They acknowledged that they had taken no part in the healing that had occurred. The Lord received all of the glory!

This miracle has stood the test for more than five years now. No trace of that growth has reappeared. I have thanked the Lord a hundred times for the healing, for the victory over fear, and for the continuing demonstration of the power of bold Bible living.

It has been many years since God first led us to pioneer the message of bold Bible living on our radio broadcasts. It has meant a great deal in my own life, for it has been through this knowledge of God's Word that I have learned to live as the Bible says in Romans 8:37—as *more than conquerors through Him who loved us.*

The Faith Walk

I once believed that if I could trust the Lord for my finances, then I could really be classed among the faith folks. As days went by and years multiplied, faith began to take on a wider scope, and I began to see how small a thing it was to trust for money alone.

Then, I trusted Him for my body. I saw that "*by His stripes we are healed*" (Isaiah 53:5). It was a glad sense of relief from the fears that had held me in the past.

Then, one day, I saw that my God was a God of faith, and all of life was faith. I saw how little a place sensory knowledge had in the scheme of things. I saw its limitations. And next to its limitations, I saw the limitlessness of faith.

Then, the Scriptures that I had read for years and thought that I understood became illumined with a light that thrilled me. I saw that in the finished work of Christ, every need of man had been met.

It was not about getting my healing. My healing had already been accomplished. It was not about getting strength to meet the obligations of the day. That strength was already mine. It was not about acquiring wisdom. Jesus became for me wisdom from God. (See 1 Corinthians 1:30.)

It was no longer prayers of desperation. It was quiet, confident talking over the day's work. It was not saying, "Lord, give me money to meet my bills." I knew that He would supply every need of mine. It was not praying for strength. He was "*the strength of my life*" (Psalm 27:1).

I discovered that the following passage in James 5 was referring to the Christian who was walking in the realm of the senses, who had never learned to walk in the realm of the Spirit. "*Is anyone among you sick? Let him call for the elders of the church, and let them pray over him, anointing him with oil in the name of the Lord*" (James 5:14).

"*Call for the elders*" was in the realm of the senses. I have stepped out of the senses and into the realm of the Spirit. I can now walk in the works prepared for me. Healing and blessing, breaking the power of demons over men's bodies, were all settled and accomplished. All I needed to do was use it.

It is like going to the closet to get a suit of clothes that is hanging there. I simply put it on and go about my work. Now, I put on the abilities, the grace, the strength, the wisdom, and the love that is necessary to meet life's problems.

Is This Promise True?

Mark 9:14–27 contains the story of the father with the epileptic child. The disciples were not able to give him deliverance. The father brought him to Jesus saying, "*If you are able to do anything, have pity on us and help us.' Jesus said to him, 'If you are able!—All things can be done for the one who believes*'" (verses 22–23 NRSV).

Here is the limitlessness of this thing; here is the challenge to everyone who reads this Word. It seems a pitiable thing that we even try to have faith. It shows how theoretical Christianity has dominated us and kept us in weakness, kept us in the realm of theory and speculation, in the realm of the world's mind rather than coming to the Word of God as little children.

Men have formulated their creeds and locked Jesus in them, so all they have is a creed Christ, or a theoretical Christ, or perhaps a historical Christ. The living Jesus, untrammeled by creed, can be approached now, and He is whispering to your heart, "All things are possible to you."

The word *believer* really means "a believing one." This throws added light on it. "A believing one" is a child of God. Then, all things are possible to the children of God. All things now belong to us.

When we were born again, we came into the family and became joint heirs with Christ. This is of great value to us. All things are possible to the sons and daughters of God, to those who have come into the family.

Be Strong in the Lord

Success in the divine life and success in the commercial life are both faith ventures. No one knows what tomorrow will bring forth in the commercial world. A fire may burn your building, or the bank that holds your money may fail. A customer who owes you enough to wreck you may go bankrupt.

But, if you trust in the Lord, you will not fail. "*Be strong in the Lord and in the power of His might*" (Ephesians 6:10). It does not tell you to be strong in your own resources but in the strength of God's might.

"*Watch, stand fast in the faith, be brave, be strong*" (1 Corinthians 16:13). Here is the challenge of love. You are to swing free from the theories of men and rest absolutely upon the Word of God, "*that He would grant you, according to the riches of His glory, to be strengthened with might through His Spirit in the inner man*" (Ephesians 3:16). Strengthened with God's strength, empowered with God's ability in that inner man, you will stand steadfast and immovable. (See 1 Corinthians 15:58.)

"Strengthened with all might, according to His glorious power, for all patience and longsuffering with joy" (Colossians 1:11). That person cannot fail. That person is a victor at the beginning of the fight.

Let us come back to our first verse: *"Be strong in the Lord"* (Ephesians 6:10). Have all the education and training you can get, but remember that your strength is in the Lord. *"For it is God who works in you both to will and to do for His good pleasure"* (Philippians 2:13). You are trusting in the God on the inside.

Bold Bible Living

Whatis bold Bible living? What does it mean?

First, bold Bible living means living with a capital *L*. *"He who has the Son has life"* (1 John 5:12). When we receive Christ as Lord and Savior, God gives us *life* abundant (see John 10:10) and everlasting (see John 3:16).

Second, we live by the Bible. Jesus taught us how to really live: *"Man shall not live by bread alone, but by every word that proceeds from the mouth of God"* (Matthew 4:4). My constant appeal in the ministry is to live by God's Word. That is Bible living.

Third, the Lord clearly led us to emphasize *bold* Bible living. In studying the Scriptures concerning bold Bible living, we discover a tremendous promise of God: every one of us can be as bold as a lion!

Why? Because *"the righteous are bold as a lion"* (Proverbs 28:1). Who are the righteous? All born-again Christians. How? By faith in Jesus Christ! We have no righteousness of our own that can please God, but God made Jesus to become sin for us, so that we might become the righteousness of God in Christ. (See 2 Corinthians 5:21.) Yes, we are the righteous of the Lord. And the righteous are as bold as lions.

What does it mean to be "*bold as a lion*"? Primarily, it means having four things: confidence, courage, fearlessness, and daring.

Confidence in Christ, not ourselves, that enables us to shout, "*I can do all things through Christ who strengthens me*" (Philippians 4:13).

Courage, the same Bible courage that characterized all of the righteous ones in the Bible. Consider the deeds of such men as Daniel, David, Elijah, Abraham, Joshua, and Moses, to name only a few.

Fearlessness, the ability of God that enables us to live free from fear all our days. "*For God has not given us a spirit of fear, but of power and of love and of a sound mind*" (2 Timothy 1:7).

Daring to act on the Word of God, to do what God says we can do.

These are four distinct qualities, yet they harmonize together. It is difficult to have one without possessing all four of them. The Word abounds with challenging truths to assure us that God gives these qualities and then expects us to use them. The Lord promises:

Fear not, for I am with you; be not dismayed, for I am your God. (Isaiah 41:10)

In quietness and confidence shall be your strength. (Isaiah 30:15)

Be strong and of good courage; do not be afraid, nor be dismayed, for the LORD your God is with you wherever you go. (Joshua 1:9)

This is bold living: being courageous under all adversities and learning that triumph goes to those who practice this truth. It is being able to say with David, *"Though an army may encamp against me, my heart shall not fear; though war should rise against me, in this I will be confident"* (Psalm 27:3).

In May 1967, I was in Israel. When we came to that area where the Israelites were in array against the Philistines, my imagination vividly recalled the great event.

If a man ever displayed courage under fire, it was David in that hour. The whole army of Israel was terrified by the giant Goliath. No man could do battle with him. In fact, they were all cowards in his presence and in the face of his humiliating taunts against Israel. So overwhelming were the odds against the Israelite army that no man would even attempt to "save face" in that time of crisis.

Yet we see David step out on that field of battle and challenge the giant who laughed at him. David was no coward. God had given him victories in the past against such formidable foes as a lion and a bear. This young man had courage, and courage was the needed quality here.

By the help of his God, David conquered the giant that day. What were his secrets? First, he believed in his heart that he could conquer Goliath, and he boldly declared the same. We, too, must confess our faith, confess the Scriptures, and boldly affirm that what God has spoken is ours. Second, David's courage was because of the name of the Lord. David declared, "*I come to you in the name of the LORD*" (1 Samuel 17:45). Our strength is in His name. Remember: "*The name of the LORD is a strong tower; the righteous run to it and are safe*" (Proverbs 18:10).

An evangelist friend of mine told me an amazing story of a man who exhibited bold Bible living and courage in the Lord under very adverse circumstances. The story went like this:

"Years ago, in a terrible blizzard, a Spirit-filled farmer was stranded many miles from home. His car windshield was freezing over, and the wipers wouldn't work. The heater was broken. He was in a desperate condition.

"This man told the Lord, 'Now, Lord, You know that I am many miles from my home. My wife is there without sufficient food. Lord, if You let me stay here, I'll freeze to death in a short time, and Mama will starve if I don't get home with the food.' Then, the man did something daring. He said, 'Lord, You know that I can't see anything at all, so

I'm going to start this car and commit it into Your hands to guide it.'

"This earnest Christian man started the car and drove it down those country roads, unable to see anything, just turning the steering wheel as he was led by the Spirit of God. Mile after mile, he drove along by spiritual radar, turning curves and corners when he felt he should do so.

"Suddenly, the car came to a dead stop. The farmer looked down and saw that the ignition had been turned off. For a moment, he was concerned and told the Lord so. 'Lord, You know this isn't my home. You have brought me thus far, but You can't let me stop here.' He looked out the window to survey his location when suddenly the express train went whizzing by. Had the car not stopped right when it did, he would have been on the tracks when the train passed!

"The man bowed his head and said, 'Thank You, Lord. You knew more about the situation than I did.' The man turned on the ignition again, started the car, and later that evening arrived at his farm safe and sound."

That is bold Bible living—moving out boldly in the face of adverse circumstances and trusting the Lord to uphold you. "*The people who know their God shall be strong, and carry out great exploits*" (Daniel 11:32). I'm sold on being bold, because those who are bold do exploits in the name of the Lord.

The Laws of Success

Every man is born with the ability to do good with his life. It is his first business to find out what he is adapted for. Stir the ambition of the child by wise counsel and the right kind of reading.

Moses fought his call for forty years and finally yielded to it. His debate with God in Exodus 3–4 should be pondered by every thinking person.

"So the Lord said to [Moses], *'What is that in your hand?' He said, 'A rod'"* (Exodus 4:2). It was this rod that God empowered and used to deliver Israel out of Egypt. The thing in your hand that seems so commonplace, when filled with God's power, can be a mighty instrument. What do you have in your hand?

"With God nothing will be impossible" (Luke 1:37). You have the Word of God in your hand. It is the mightiest weapon, the most tremendous instrument ever known. *"He who is in you is greater than he who is in the world"* (1 John 4:4). You have God in you, yet you tell me that you cannot do things. You can!

"Whatever you ask in My name, that I will do, that the Father may be glorified in the Son" (John 14:13). You have the name of Jesus with which you may command disease and sickness to leave the bodies of men.

Jesus said, *"Whatever you ask the Father in My name He will give you"* (John 16:23). You not only have the name to break the power of disease and sin and Satan's dominion, but you also can reach the very throne of God and stand there as a conqueror.

"You Will Have Good Success"

Read God's words to Joshua: *"As I was with Moses, so I will be with you. I will not leave you nor forsake you"* (Joshua 1:5). What strong consolation! There is something so hearty, so strong, and so victorious in God's counsel to Joshua that my heart unconsciously returns to it again and again.

> *This Book of the Law shall not depart from your mouth, but you shall meditate in it day and night, that you may observe to do according to all that is written in it. For then you will make your way prosperous, and then you will have good success.* (Joshua 1:8)

Here is the secret of spiritual success, financial success, and physical success. Devote yourself to know the Book and to know Him who inspired the Book. Find out His will; then, swing free and live in it and do it.

With God, life becomes a drama, a romance. After a while, a sense of His omnipotence will dominate your spirit. Philippians 4:13 is a battle-ax with which you can smash every barrier between you and success: *"I can do all things through Christ who strengthens me."*

Your success is His success; if you were to fail, it would be His failure. He is backing you, and His eye is upon you.

"I Will Not Fail You"

"I will not leave you nor forsake you" (Joshua 1:5). How those words must have thrilled that hero of God!

Remember that Moses said, *"If Your Presence does not go with us, do not bring us up from here"* (Exodus 33:15). Moses was not willing to go alone or to go with an angel. But he would go with God. And God said, *"My Presence will go with you"* (verse 14).

Later, God said to Joshua, *"As I was with Moses, so I will be with you"* (Joshua 1:5). So, when Joshua stood in front of the Jordan and saw the waters spread out before him with no bridge, no tunnel, and no fording place, he dared to say to the priests, *"Take up the ark of the covenant and cross over before the people"* (Joshua 3:6). He knew that the waters must give way.

Then, the miracle of miracles happened. As though a huge sword had dropped and separated

88

the waters, part of them rushed down toward the sea, and the other part was held back by the invisible hand of omnipotence and the command of man. Joshua's words had power. They were filled with authority.

God has said, "*I am ready to perform My word*" (Jeremiah 1:12). When Jesus said, "*Whatever you ask in My name, that I will do*" (John 14:13), He was also promising to watch over that word and make it good.

You may dare to lay your hands on the sick and say, "In the name of Jesus, disease must leave this body." Your words are filled with divine authority, for your words are His words. Do not fear, for He is with you.

How to Receive Guidance from God

> *Trust in the LORD with all your heart, and lean not on your own understanding; in all your ways acknowledge Him, and He shall direct your paths.* (Proverbs 3:5–6)

> *Your word is a lamp to my feet and a light to my path.* (Psalm 119:105)

All guidance must be in harmony with the Word, never apart from it. The Holy Spirit always uses the Word: "*The sword of the Spirit, which is the word of God*" (Ephesians 6:17). For instance, the Holy Spirit never leads a Christian to marry a non-Christian, for that would be a violation of His Word. "*Do not be unequally yoked together with unbelievers*" (2 Corinthians 6:14). The Holy Spirit *never* leads a true Christian to walk in darkness. As Jesus said, "*I am the light of the world. He who follows Me shall not walk in darkness*" (John 8:12).

We should not make guidance complicated. "*A man's heart plans his way, but the Lord directs his steps*" (Proverbs 16:9). We must submit to His lord-ship over our lives. "*Trust in the Lord with all your heart*" (Proverbs 3:5). Confess it: "Jesus is Lord; I trust Him with all my heart."

We must resist the enemy by using the authority of Jesus to silence his voice. "*Resist the devil and he will flee from you*" (James 4:7). Because we are Jesus' sheep, we can expect to have His guidance. "*My sheep hear My voice, and I know them, and they follow Me*" (John 10:27).

Allow God to speak in the way He chooses. Pray as Samuel did: "*Speak, for Your servant hears*" (1 Samuel 3:10). God may choose to speak with an audible voice (see Exodus 3:4–5), by dreams (see Matthew 2:13, 22), or by visions (see Isaiah 6; Revelation 1:9–17). One of the most usual ways God gives guidance is revealed in Isaiah 30:21: "*Your ears shall hear a word behind you, saying, 'This is the way, walk in it,' whenever you turn to the right hand or whenever you turn to the left.*"

Get your own leading from God, but realize that the Lord may use others to confirm your guidance. At the same time, beware of counterfeit guidance.

A True Story of Guidance in China

There is a story from Communist China about a Christian woman who was working in a mining operation. One of her duties was to blow the whistle that alerted the miners when it was time to leave the mine for lunch or for the day. Faithfully, she performed her duties as instructed by the Communist leadership.

One day, this woman experienced a strong inner urge to blow the whistle a full hour before lunchtime. There was a great conflict within her. Her instructions were to wait for another hour, and yet she sensed the Holy Spirit's strong urging to do it right now. To disobey orders might lead to loss of work—and possibly other consequences. What should she do?

The decision was made, for the impulse was strong. Indeed, she felt she would be disobeying God if she didn't blow the whistle. A full hour before lunch, she blew the whistle, and all the workers came out of the mine. When the last one emerged, the mine collapsed.

The news about the mine collapse spread quickly around the area. Communist officials and supervisors of the mine operation came to the accident site. They soon discovered that every worker was accounted for and that everyone was safe and sound. The hero of the day was the young woman who had called the workers out from the subterranean passages. An interrogation followed.

"Who told you to blow the whistle?" they asked. She felt compelled to tell exactly what had happened—how the Holy Spirit had urged her to sound the life-saving alarm. Workers, families, friends, and officials all realized that almighty God had intervened and prevented a major mining disaster. And this led to a widespread revival of the gospel of Jesus Christ in that area.

You, too, can be guided by God. You can hear His voice!

Miracles and Healing

What Is a Miracle?

I once asked a class if they could define a miracle. I shall never forget the looks on the faces of those young men and women. I asked, "Isn't it Christ revealing the creative energy of God, acting in the physical realm?"

A miracle is God intruding into the sensory realm. It is the Spirit dominating physical forces. When God heals a person, He is making normal what the adversary has distorted. A miracle is God restoring what Satan has destroyed. Jesus Himself was a miracle. His incarnation was miraculous. The senses cannot understand it. It belongs to the spiritual realm.

His miracles were all beyond human reasoning. He made a limb that had been amputated become whole again. He healed the leper and made that diseased flesh become pure and wholesome again. He raised from the dead a man who had been in the grave for nearly a week; his body had begun to decay, but it became perfectly whole.

Jesus spoke, and the very fish of the sea obeyed Him. He commanded a storm to cease, and the water became calm and peaceful. He walked on the water. How could He do it? He was God incarnate.

Are miracles a part of the plan of God for us today? The church began with miracles. The new creation is without a doubt the master miracle. Healing the sick is miraculous. Walking upon the sea was a miracle. But when God imparts His nature to a man like Saul of Tarsus, whose hands were wet with the blood of men and women he had slain, and in a single moment makes him a new creation, that is the miracle of all miracles.

Creating a universe is a miracle. But recreating a child of the devil and making him God's own son, imparting to him God's own love nature—to me, that is the crowning miracle of all.

When you take the miraculous out of Christianity, you have nothing but philosophy, and philosophy provides only sensory knowledge that cannot transform people. Christianity is a miracle. It is God's intrusion into the human realm.

Being Miracle-Minded

The world has become doubt-minded. In the higher realms of education, it is a mark of scholarship to put a question mark after every sentence and to challenge all the old landmarks. It is an unhealthy mental condition, because continual questions are a sign of weakness.

Doubt has never been a sign of strength. It isn't doubting something, but believing something, that makes men strong. Doubts always bring unhealthy reactions. Faith always has healthy reactions.

Blessed is the man who becomes faith-minded toward God and faith-minded toward the Bible, who reaches the place where doubt is unwanted and abhorred. He comes to the place where faith is cultivated, nurtured, and welcome.

The next step beyond that is to become miracle-minded. Jesus was miracle-minded. Elijah was miracle-minded. Paul and Peter were miracle-minded. Once a person or a people becomes miracle-minded, you will see scenes that were common to the apostolic church. But among a doubt-minded and world-minded people, you see nothing of this character.

Faith-mindedness and miracle-mindedness come from a walk with the Lord Jesus. I question if anyone can walk very closely to the Lord, making the Bible the center of his life and Jesus the Lord of his life, without becoming miracle-minded.

You see, the farther we go from the Master, the dimmer our faith grows. The nearer we come to Him, the more clearly we see Him with the eyes of faith. If you are in the place where doubts dominate you, you are a long way from the Master. If you are where faith dominates you, you are walking close to Him.

Unbelief, then, can be called far-ness. Faith can be called near-ness. Miracle-mindedness makes prayer a business proposition: you are making investments of time and you are drawing dividends and thoughts in your prayer life. You are seeing God work.

Our people have become faith-minded. Quite a large number have become miracle-minded, and, as a result, every week we see staggering miracles performed. We see miracles that our scientific friends say are impossible. We agree with them. They are impossible, humanly speaking; but *"all things are possible to him who believes"* (Mark 9:23), or to the miracle-minded person, and we are growing increasingly miracle-minded. We are finding that what God said is true, and that what God did in Christ is real.

So I suggest this to my readers: ask the Lord to help you to so live in the realm of the Word, in the faith realm, that you will grow miracle-minded. Don't misunderstand me. The great world outside lives in the reason realm. You can't live in the reason realm and please God.

You might ask, then, for what purpose your reason is given to you. It is to be sanctified by the Spirit and brought into captivity by the Lord Jesus so that you can think God's thoughts after Him. (See 2 Corinthians 10:5.) It was never given to you to cultivate doubt, fear, and skepticism, or to rebel against the Word of God and the mind of Christ. So bring that unruly reasoning faculty into subjection to Christ.

The Supernatural

Supernatural—the very word breathes of miracles. Christianity itself is supernatural. It is the union of Deity and humanity. That union was first manifested in the Man of Galilee, and then again on the day of Pentecost, when 120 men and women were united with Deity.

The new birth is a miracle. It is supernatural. It is partaking of the nature of God. Every child of God is a miracle. When the Spirit comes into a person's body and makes it His home, a miracle has taken place. That person is now capable of living in the Spirit realm, where Jesus lived when He was on earth.

The faith realm, the love realm, and the Spirit realm represent the plain on which we meet God. The one who walks by faith and not by reason or feelings is walking in the supernatural. The one who walks in love lives in the realm above reason. That is supernatural.

Natural man is selfish. The love of Jesus takes us out of the realm of selfishness and into the realm of God. The man who walks in the Spirit is walking in the realm above reason or physical evidences. He may experience them, but he is not in their realm.

"Fear not, for I am with you; be not dismayed, for I am your God. I will strengthen you, yes, I will help you, I will uphold you with My righteous right hand" (Isaiah 41:10). Here is God actually participating in our daily activities. He is a partner with us in all that we are and do.

He is making us one with Himself. His strength becomes our strength. His life becomes our life. His wisdom, love, and quietness are ours. We are utterly identified with Him. He becomes a part of everything we do, and we can surely say, *"I can do all things through Christ who strengthens me"* (Philippians 4:13).

It takes us out of the realm of weakness, fear, and inability, and it moves us into the realm of His own ability. We become supermen and superwomen. By His grace, we know that *"He who is in you is greater than he who is in the world"* (1 John 4:4). We fearlessly undertake the impossible.

We are not counting on our weaknesses, our limitations, our lack of knowledge, or our lack of finances. We are counting on the One who has called us into fellowship with His Son, Jesus Christ.

How You Can Be Healed

I s it truly God's will that we receive healing for our bodies? His will is expressed in His Word, where we read, *"Beloved, I pray that you may prosper in all things and be in health, just as your soul prospers"* (3 John 2). Our loving Father expresses His wishes for us in this dynamic verse. He desires that we may prosper and be in health, even as our souls prosper.

Prerequisite to Healing

Of course, the most important thing is to make sure that we are prospering in our souls. That is a prerequisite to healing. The healing of our bodies begins with the healing of our souls. Soul prosperity means confessing and forsaking known sin.

> *If I regard iniquity in my heart, the LORD will not hear.*　　　　　　　　(Psalm 66:18)

> *He who covers his sins will not prosper, but whoever confesses and forsakes them will have mercy.*　　　　　　　　(Proverbs 28:13)

Behold, the LORD's hand is not shortened, that
it cannot save; nor His ear heavy, that it can-
not hear. But your iniquities have separated
you from your God; and your sins have hidden
His face from you, so that He will not hear.
(Isaiah 59:1–2)

Sometimes, we may fail to receive healing—not
because of the shortness of the Lord's hand or the
heaviness of His ear, but because sin has caused a
break in our fellowship with Him. If so, obey His
Word, which says, *"If we confess our sins, He is faith-*
ful and just to forgive us our sins and to cleanse us
from all unrighteousness" (1 John 1:9). Then, you will
be on the right basis to believe God for healing.

Since healing begins within, let us consider another Scripture.

And whenever you stand praying, if you have
anything against anyone, forgive him, that
your Father in heaven may also forgive you
your trespasses. But if you do not forgive, nei-
ther will your Father in heaven forgive your
trespasses.   (Mark 11:25–26)

Before your prayers for healing will be effective,
you must be sure that you hold no grudge or un-
forgiving spirit against anyone. Ask yourself, *Have*
I allowed a hurt to cause resentment within my
heart? Do I harbor—perhaps unknowingly—ill will
against anyone? If so, your prayers for healing will
not be answered. Call upon God and depend upon

His unfailing grace to enable you to forgive every offense committed against you.

Again, healing begins with an internal, spiritual cleansing.

> *Search me, O God, and know my heart; try me, and know my anxieties; and see if there is any wicked way in me, and lead me in the way everlasting.* (Psalm 139:23–24)

> *Who can understand his errors? Cleanse me from secret faults. Keep back Your servant also from presumptuous sins; let them not have dominion over me....Let the words of my mouth and the meditation of my heart be acceptable in Your sight, O LORD, my strength and my Redeemer.* (Psalm 19:12–14)

You Have What You Say

It may be that a wrong confession is causing your downfall spiritually and physically. If so, you can resolve with David, "*I will guard my ways, lest I sin with my tongue*" (Psalm 39:1). It may be that your words need cleansing because your heart needs cleansing. Jesus said, "*Out of the abundance of the heart the mouth speaks*" (Matthew 12:34). Seek from the Lord a clean heart, and then your words will be pure, edifying, and ministering grace to your hearers. (See Ephesians 4:29.)

The words that we speak are of extreme importance in determining whether we enjoy healing and health or sickness and disease. Jesus said, *"He will have whatever he says"* (Mark 11:23). If we are always talking about our aches and pains, then aches and pains will be what we have. But if we talk about the goodness of the Lord, praising Him for His healing power, we can enjoy divine health.

Our tongues determine whether we have health or sickness. *"The tongue of the wise promotes health"* (Proverbs 12:18). If we discipline our tongues to confess, *"By His stripes we are healed"* (Isaiah 53:5), then our tongues are the instrument of health. *"Pleasant words are like a honeycomb, sweetness to the soul and health to the bones"* (Proverbs 16:24). Pleasant words—words pleasing to God—minister health to the believer.

"Death and life are in the power of the tongue" (Proverbs 18:21). The tongue can produce death. How? *"You are snared by the words of your mouth; you are taken* [captive] *by the words of your mouth"* (Proverbs 6:2). If you speak words about sickness rather than about God's healing power, then your lips are the snare of your soul. (See Proverbs 18:7.)

"A wholesome tongue is a tree of life" (Proverbs 15:4). We know that the Tree of Life will be *"for the healing of the nations"* (Revelation 22:2). *"The tongue of the wise uses knowledge rightly"* (Proverbs 15:2). We

should have full knowledge of the Scriptures that teach healing so that we can affirm them with our tongues. "*Bless the LORD, O my soul…who heals all your diseases*" (Psalm 103:2–3). With our tongues, we will always speak God's healing words, for they are "*health to all their flesh*" (Proverbs 4:22).

The Basis for Our Healing

Healing is based on the finished work of Jesus at Calvary.

> *But He was wounded for our transgressions, He was bruised for our iniquities; the chastisement for our peace was upon Him, and by His stripes we are healed.* (Isaiah 53:5)

> *He cast out the spirits with a word, and healed all who were sick, that it might be fulfilled which was spoken by Isaiah the prophet, saying: "He Himself took our infirmities and bore our sicknesses."* (Matthew 8:16–17)

Jesus purchased our healing at the price of great suffering. Tradition tells us that the whip with which He was beaten was an ugly weapon. Tiny pieces of metal were woven into each of the nine leather thongs. The Roman scourging with this deadly whip surpassed all other methods of cruel punishment—it was worse than crucifixion itself. It was so frightful that the condemned one often died while being beaten with this instrument of torture.

Our Savior's hands were tied high above His head while a Roman soldier cruelly lashed Him with the whip. Thirty-nine times, its jagged thongs gouged His flesh. In those lashes, which cut His back to ribbons, our Lord bore all of our misery, pains, and sicknesses. He suffered the agony of every known disease so that we need not suffer. It was through these stripes that healing became ours.

David Bush, a missionary to Japan, was stricken with a disease that threatened his life. While lying on his bed in intense pain, he remembered God's promises and claimed his healing. The next morning, he rose up from his bed, completely well.

Our authority for healing is based on what Christ has done, and we can claim this healing in the name of Jesus. Know the value of your confession of faith. Declare boldly, "By His stripes I am healed." Then, begin to do the things you couldn't do before.

Don't waver in your faith, or you will receive nothing from the Lord. (See James 1:6–8.) Resist the devil in the name of Jesus. Continue to praise the Lord with all your heart, thanking Him for healing you.

If You Need Healing, Speak These Words Aloud

- "No matter what symptoms are present, by His stripes I am healed."
- "Regardless of what others may say about my health, by His stripes I am healed."
- "In spite of past experiences, by His stripes I am healed."

- "When pain strikes my body, by His stripes I am healed."
- "Wherever I am, by His stripes I am healed."
- "Regardless of how I feel, by His stripes I am healed."
- "When symptoms reappear, by His stripes I am healed."

The Origin of Disease

It is of the utmost importance that we know where diseases originate in order for us to find a remedy. We are sure that disease is not a part of God's plan and that it came to man as the result of spiritual death, which came to him at the fall.

It is very important that we understand God's view of man in our study of disease. All through the Scriptures, He speaks of man in a different way than we do today. The study of psychology has made man a mental being to us, but God does not look upon him that way. Man is a spirit being; he has a soul, intellect, and reasoning faculties; and he lives in a body.

When God speaks of a man, He speaks of the whole man—spirit, soul, and body. When He speaks of saving, healing, or blessing, He is not speaking of just blessing man mentally, physically, or spiritually, but blessing him as a whole man. Nowhere does God separate man spiritually and physically as we do.

It is evident from the teachings of the Master that disease and sickness are the work of the adversary. God is the logical healer. A passage in Luke 13 gives us an illustration.

There was a woman who had a spirit of infirmity eighteen years, and was bent over and could in no way raise herself up. But when Jesus saw her, He called her to Him and said to her, "Woman, you are loosed from your infirmity." And He laid His hands on her, and immediately she was made straight, and glorified God.
(verses 11–13)

This healing raised up a storm of protest because it was the Sabbath, but Jesus answered His critics, *"Ought not this woman, being a daughter of Abraham, whom Satan has bound; think of it; for eighteen years, be loosed from this bond on the Sabbath?"* (verse 16). Jesus declared that Satan had bound this woman and held her in bondage. Previously, He had said,

I say to you, My friends, do not be afraid of those who kill the body, and after that have no more that they can do. But I will show you whom you should fear: Fear Him who, after He has killed, has power to cast into hell.
(Luke 12:4–5)

Satan had the authority to kill, and he had authority to cast people into hell. Here, Satan is shown to have the power of death:

> *As the children have partaken of flesh and blood, [Jesus] Himself likewise shared in the same, that through death He might destroy him who had the power of death, that is, the devil.*
> (Hebrews 2:14)

In this passage, the author is speaking of Jesus' substitutionary sacrifice. Jesus conquered the one who had the authority of death.

We know that from the very beginning of Jesus' public ministry, He directly encountered demons. As an illustration, take Matthew 4:23. This was at the beginning of Jesus' public ministry, right after He was tempted in the wilderness: "*Jesus went about all Galilee, teaching in their synagogues, preaching the gospel of the kingdom, and healing all kinds of sickness and all kinds of disease among the people.*"

I used to wonder why so much space was given to the healing of the demoniac of the Gergesenes.

> *When He had come to the other side, to the country of the Gergesenes, there met Him two demon-possessed men, coming out of the tombs, exceedingly fierce, so that no one could pass that way. And suddenly they cried out, saying,*

> *"What have we to do with You, Jesus, You Son of God? Have You come here to torment us before the time?"* (Matthew 8:28–29)

That demoniac was possessed through his lips, and the demon was speaking through his lips. This story is very important, or else it would not have been recorded three times in the Gospels.

I remember reading years ago that one of the outstanding medical authorities on this subject declared that the largest portion of the insane gave positive proof that they were possessed by evil spirits.

We have had many experiences with this kind of possession and have seen many people delivered. Men have grown out of the idea of demons, and that gives the adversary a greater advantage over them.

"God anointed Jesus of Nazareth with the Holy Spirit and with power, who went about doing good and healing all who were oppressed by the devil, for God was with Him" (Acts 10:38). These people were healed not only of demon possession, but also of the adversary's work—sickness and disease, hunger and lack.

In Acts 16:18, there is an account of Paul casting a demon out of a girl. *"Paul, greatly annoyed, turned and said to the spirit, 'I command you in the name of Jesus Christ to come out of her.' And he came out that very hour."*

Everything that brings misery, pain, hunger, or lack to man is directly or indirectly the work of the adversary. *"He who sins is of the devil, for the devil has sinned from the beginning. For this purpose the Son of God was manifested, that He might destroy the works of the devil"* (1 John 3:8).

If our findings are right and Satan is the author of disease, then the logical healer is God. We recognize all the strides of advancement that medical science has made, and we thank God for them. But, in spite of these advancements, sickness and disease have continued to gain. New hospitals are being built continually. Private sanatoriums are everywhere. A large percentage of the homes in our land have someone who is sick or ailing.

But when sick people went to Jesus by the thousands, He healed every one of them. The same thing was true of the disciples as they worked among the Jews. They all were healed. We know it is the Father's will that all be healed, because sickness is from the adversary, and in the finished work of Christ, the power of Satan was brought to nothing.

God's Cure for Your Cares

The Bible is a book of cures for all diseases. The great salvation that Jesus provided offers a cure for everything the devil has done to you.

There are diseases of the spirit as well as of the body. Many of these spiritual diseases can, if not cured early, lead to physical illnesses. Listed below are some of these spiritual diseases and the scriptural "prescription" for them.

Worry. Multitudes of people go through life needlessly worrying. Worry can't help you; it never solved a problem, paid a bill, or healed a sickness. Jesus asked, *"Which of you by worrying can add one cubit to his stature?"* (Matthew 6:27). In other words, what will you gain by worrying? Jesus said, *"Do not worry about your life, what you will eat or what you will drink; nor about your body, what you will put on. Is not life more than food and the body more than clothing?"* (verse 25). Then, He gave the sure cure for worry: *"But seek first the kingdom of God and His righteousness, and all these things shall be added to you"* (verse 33). When your heart is fixed upon the things of the Spirit, you can be confident in the fact that God will supply all your needs.

Guilt. Are you burdened down with feelings of guilt? Are you carrying a load of sin? If your life is filled with sin, if your heart is not right with God, there is a cure. *"The blood of Jesus Christ His Son cleanses us from all sin.…If we confess our sins, He is faithful and just to forgive us our sins and to cleanse us from all unrighteousness"* (1 John 1:7, 9). Confess your sins today and accept Christ's forgiveness for your life. Then you can live a life free from the condemnation and guilt of sin. *"Blessed is he whose transgression is forgiven, whose sin is covered"* (Psalm 32:1).

Nervousness. If you suffer from nervousness, you are greatly hindered from enjoying life to its fullest. You are not walking in the joy that God has for you. Do you fret over problems? Do certain people or situations cause you anxiety and produce nervousness? Read Psalm 91 in its entirety. This magnificent psalm begins, *"He who dwells in the secret place of the Most High shall abide under the shadow of the Almighty"* (verse 1). You won't be nervous or upset if you learn how to dwell in God's secret place. As you learn to live in the presence of God, you will enjoy His perfect joy. "*In Your presence is fullness of joy; at Your right hand are pleasures forevermore*" (Psalm 16:11).

Insomnia. Are you bothered by sleeplessness? It is startling to realize the vast number of people who are robbed of sleep every night. Let me prescribe Psalm 4:8: "*I will both lie down in peace, and sleep; for You alone, O LORD, make me dwell in safety.*" Isn't that a wonderful verse? Lie down, then, and in the name of Jesus, you can go to sleep. Enjoy the rest that God has provided for you. Another promise in His Word is found in Psalm 127:2: "*He gives His beloved sleep.*" No longer do you need to resort to sleeping pills, for you can take the Lord's sure Word for your sleep.

The "Blues." Have you ever felt "blue"? This is nothing more than a spirit of depression and despondency that grips you and causes you to be heavyhearted. The next time you feel this way, read Psalm 42:5: "*Why are you cast down, O my soul? And why are you disquieted within me? Hope in God, for I shall yet praise Him for the help of His countenance.*" A sure cure for a case of the blues is to sing forth the praises of God.

Fear and Anxiety. I have been astonished to discover how many of God's people are oppressed by fear. When we consider what an insidious monster fear is, we must seek freedom from its destructiveness by looking to God's Word. Fear can produce misery,

116

defeat, bondage, and destruction. *"Fear involves torment"* (1 John 4:18), and it produces in kind—what you fear will come upon you. (See Job 3:25.) *"The fear of man brings a snare"* (Proverbs 29:25). The Bible doesn't call your fear "a mental quirk" but rather defines it as "a spirit." *"God has not given us a spirit of fear, but of power and of love and of a sound mind"* (2 Timothy 1:7).

Confess these words of David: *"The Lord is my light and my salvation; whom shall I fear? The Lord is the strength of my life; of whom shall I be afraid?"* (Psalm 27:1). If you let the Lord be your life, your light, your strength, and your salvation, you need have no fear. What can hurt you if the Lord is within you? Who can harm you if you follow Christ? What disease or plague can affect your life if Christ has control? Be delivered from the fear of death, the fear of disease, the fear of calamity, and the fear of old age. Whatever you fear, realize that God has not given you that spirit of fear. It comes from the devil, and in Jesus' name, you can cast out the spirit of fear.

God indeed has the cure for all your cares. Nothing can take from you the tranquility of God's blessed care and peace in your soul. Nothing can separate you from God. Nothing can cheat you out of His blessings, His healing, and His deliverance if you will believe and obey His Word.

He Can Be Touched

One day, when Jesus was surrounded by a great assembly of people, there came to the fringe of that crowd a sickly, broken-hearted woman. Her money was gone. Her strength was gone. She knew that she did not have the physical strength to force her way through to reach the Healer, so she dropped to her knees and crawled through the crowd.

With hands trembling and tears falling, she forced her way through until she could see the hem of His garment. She lifted her hands and strained until the ends of her fingers touched it. Down through her fingers, her hand, the life flowed. Life thrilled the heart and lungs, and every fiber of her body felt electric. She became well—suddenly, marvelously well!

She rose to her feet and stood amazed in the crowd. No one knew it. Finally, the strange Man turned and asked, "Who touched Me?" Peter answered, "Master, the throng of people were pressing You." And He answered, "Someone made a demand upon My power. I felt it go out of Me."

And the woman, filled with unspeakable joy, cried, "Master, it was I!" Coming forward, she fell on her face, telling Him the bitter story of years of suffering, privation, and heartache. Jesus, raising her up, said, "Woman, your faith has made you whole." (See Luke 8:43–48.)

She had touched Jesus; oh, blessed touch—the touch of faith! Can we touch Him today? Can we come with our diseased, sin-scarred bodies, our sin-prisoned spirits, our blinded souls? Can we come and touch Him?

Yes! The Scriptures tell us that He can be "*touched with the feeling of our infirmities*" (Hebrews 4:15 KJV). Today, you can touch Him, no matter what the bonds are that hold you captive. You can touch Him and be made free.

I have seen sinners touch Him and find salvation and eternal life. I have seen the sick touch Him and find their healing. I have seen those who were in financial need touch Him and find relief. There is not one need in our lives that He cannot fill.

Reach out your hand today. If you cannot touch more than the hem of His garment, He will hear your voice, feel your touch, and heal your need. Touch Him today!

The Children's Bread

In Mark 7, we find the beautiful story of Jesus dealing with the Syro-Phoenician woman; we also read one of the most striking expressions that ever fell from the Master's lips.

You remember the story. Jesus was on a vacation over on the borders of Tyre and Sidon. He was trying to hide away for a little while with His disciples. He entered a house and wanted no one to know it, but He could not be hidden.

A woman, hearing that He was there, fell down at His feet and cried for help. She was a Greek by race, and she asked Him to cast a demon out of her daughter. She was a Gentile. She had no right to seek help from this Prophet who was ministering to the lost sheep of the house of Israel.

He said, *"Let the children be filled first, for it is not good to take the children's bread and throw it to the little dogs"* (Mark 7:27). The woman took her place. She looked up into His face and said, "Master, don't You know that even the little dogs under the table eat from the children's crumbs?" (See verse 28.) This touched His heart. He said, "Go, for your prayer is answered."

Jesus said something of tremendous importance in this passage. He said that healing is the children's bread. I wonder if you have ever thought about this. If that is the case, then every child of God who is sick has a right to the "children's bread."

This puts healing on a new and intensely practical plane.

Is Healing for Me?

With halting words, the ashen lips of a dying woman asked me this question: "Is healing for me?

The doctors have given me up to die; they say an operation would be of no value. Can God and will God give me back my health?"

I said, "There is only one answer to this, and only one Person can answer it." It is God in His Word. What has He said about it? Let us turn to Isaiah and read the words that have thrilled the hearts of millions.

Surely He has borne our griefs and carried our sorrows.....He was wounded for our transgressions, He was bruised for our iniquities; the chastisement for our peace was upon Him, and by His stripes we are healed. (Isaiah 53:4–5)

That was a prophecy about the Master, written several hundred years before He came. When He came, He went to the cross, and God laid upon Him not only our iniquities but also our diseases. Peter also told us, by the Holy Spirit, that we are healed by His stripes. (See 1 Peter 2:24.)

It was done. I showed this woman who had asked me the question that if Christ had borne her diseases already, she had no right to bear them too, for by bearing them, she was annulling all that Christ had done.

Then we went over the plan of redemption. We saw beyond a shadow of a doubt that Jesus had come to save men—the whole man. The body is a part of him, the soul is a part of him, and the spirit is a part of him. If God healed man, it was spirit, soul, and body that were healed. She saw it.

121

Then, I began to unfold the Scriptures, and I proved that she had a perfect redemption in Christ. It was hers, for He had died for her. It was a personal affair.

Are Miracles for Us Today?

Many people believe that the days of miracles ended with the apostolic church— that is, when the apostles died. Some boldly claim that miracles ended about A.D. 67. Yet John's gospel was not written until approximately A.D. 95, and John gave us Jesus' marvelous message in regard to the use of His name. These promises would mean nothing if it was true that the day of miracles ended with the days of the apostles.

We cannot believe that the Holy Spirit would inspire the gospel of John if it would have no application to the church. We believe that miracles belong to the church as long as it is a church.

Here are some facts. Every new birth is a miracle, and a greater miracle than the healing of any disease. Every answered prayer is a miracle. An answered prayer is a divine response to man. A miracle is divine intervention, temporarily setting aside the laws of nature.

In our ministry, miracles are the order of the day. We see cancers healed, sometimes instantaneously; we see the healing of ulcers and tumors, goiters, tuberculosis, heart disease, and other diseases too numerous to mention. If there is pain, it leaves. If there is a fever, it leaves the body. Old, chronic cases in which people have suffered for years result in healing. These are miracles.

When Jesus said to Peter, "Come," that night when the Master was walking upon the sea, it was Jesus' invitation to walk the waves with Him. Even now, He invites every believer into the realm of the supernatural, to walk the waves with Him.

Come, Walk the Waves with Me

This is love's invitation to walk with Christ in the realm of the supernatural. Jesus united the natural man with the supernatural life.

The story in Matthew 14 is one of the most significant of all the teachings in the Word. It is an account of Jesus walking on the sea, inviting Peter to come and walk with Him, and then giving a tender remonstrance when Peter failed and began to sink.

Peter wanted to walk the waves. Jesus wanted him to walk the waves. It seemed so natural to Peter when he saw the Master walking on the water that he said, "*Lord, if it is You, command me to come to You on the water*" (Matthew 14:28). Jesus uttered one word: "*Come*" (verse 29).

How far Peter walked, we do not know, but it must have been quite a long way. Then, when he saw the billows rolling, he lost sight of the Master and forgot His Word, and he began to sink.

The Master wants us to walk with Him. It is the call of grace to live in the realm of the supernatural. This walk with Christ is not natural. It is above nature. It is God lifting us into His own realm. It is above the senses. It is above the mind of the senses. It is in the realm of the Spirit. We are to walk in the Spirit and not in the realm of the senses.

Miracles are natural to this divine life. Anything short of the miraculous is to go back into the beggarly elements of the world. Jesus would not have invited Peter to walk the waves with Him if He had not planned a miraculous life for us all. For us to deny miracles today is to deny the very heart of Christianity.

Christianity without miracles is like marriage without love. Christianity without miracles is insipid and unwanted, because Christianity demands a higher type of walk than natural man can walk. The new commandment, that we love one another even as He has loved us, demands a miracle life. (See John 13:34.)

As I said, sensory knowledge has gained mastery of the church. The church as we know it today is not the body of Christ unveiled in the Pauline revelation. The body of Christ as seen through the eyes of God the Father is a supernatural body whose life depends on miracles and whose very being is miraculous.

In John 14:12, Jesus laid down the law of this new life: "*He who believes in Me, the works that I do he will do also; and greater works than these he will do, because I go to My Father.*" Then, He told us the method of the greater works in the next two verses: "*And whatever you ask in My name, that I will do, that the Father may be glorified in the Son. If you ask anything in My name, I will do it*" (verses 13–14).

The word "*ask*" in this passage can mean "demand." Now you can understand Peter's demand when speaking to the lame man at the gate called Beautiful. (See Acts 3:1–7.) The name of Jesus is to be used in casting out demons and breaking the power of Satan over lives. That is not prayer. That is our combat with invisible hosts of darkness.

In John 15:16, we are told to pray to the Father in the name of Jesus, and whatever we ask, He will give it to us. The Master intended that we walk the waves with Him. He planned that we would be independent of circumstances—so utterly one with Him that His life would dominate ours, and we could say, "*It is no longer I who live, but Christ lives in me*" (Galatians 2:20).

Romans 8:11 is a living reality: "*If the Spirit of Him who raised Jesus from the dead dwells in you, He who raised Christ from the dead will also give life to your mortal bodies through His Spirit who dwells in you.*" The whole thing is victorious, triumphant. Nowhere can we find a place for weakness and failure in this divine life.

God never planned that we should be subjugated to the forces of darkness. He never planned that Satan should reign over us.

Matthew 17:20 promises that "*nothing will be impossible for you.*" Why did He say it if He did not mean it? Why should He tantalize us with impossibilities? "*Whatever things you ask in prayer, believing, you will receive*" (Matthew 21:22). "*All things are possible to him who believes*" (Mark 9:23). That means a believer—literally, "a believing one."

In Matthew 19:26, Jesus said, "*With God all things are possible.*" We are tied up with God. We are united with Him. He dwells in us. We live in Him.

Is He merely tantalizing us when He says, "*He who is in you is greater than he who is in the world*" (1 John 4:4)? Are they idle words when He says, "*My God shall supply all your need*" (Philippians 4:19), or "*I can do all things through Christ who strengthens me*" (Philippians 4:13), or "*I am ready to perform My word*" (Jeremiah 1:12)?

Does He mean what He says? We are certain that He does. We believe that when He bids us come and walk with Him in the way of victory, in the supernatural way, in the miracle way, He means it.

127

This walking the waves with Him is the fruit of righteousness. If you are the righteousness of God and you live in defeat and failure, you give the world a wrong conception of Christianity. We who walk by faith walk in triumph in Jesus Christ.

Sickness, Health, and Healing

Someone recently told me, "I have been a good and sincere person all my life, attending church regularly and teaching a Sunday school class. I have recently learned that I have cancer, which threatens to cut my life short before I can raise my family. Do you think I have a right to be healed?"

"Most assuredly!" I responded, "But not because you have been a good and sincere person. Not even because you attend church regularly and teach a Sunday school class. And it's not even because your family needs you. Those are all noble reasons, but they are not the grounds for your claim to healing."

The only foundation for healing is through Christ's provision for you at Calvary. "*He was wounded for our transgressions, He was bruised for our iniquities; the chastisement for our peace was upon Him, and by His stripes we are healed*" (Isaiah 53:5). (See also Matthew 8:16–17.)

To receive healing, you must depend entirely on the merits of Jesus Christ, "*who Himself bore our sins in His own body on the tree, that we, having died to sins, might live for righteousness; by whose stripes you were healed"* (1 Peter 2:24). Every lash of that cruel Roman whip purchased healing for you and me.

Acting on God's Word

Some time ago, I ministered at a church in Springfield, Oregon. The Holy Spirit led me to speak on the subject of praise. After ministering this truth and leading the people into the glorious life of praise, I closed the service.

A man then approached me on the platform and said, "Brother Gossett, you have preached about the power of praise, and I am a living testimony of how the Lord responds to praise.

"Just one year ago," he went on, "I was in the intensive care unit of the hospital, dying with emphysema. The doctors told my family that I had only five minutes to live. When I realized I had such a short time to live, I decided to devote those precious minutes to praising my Lord for all His mercies and blessings I had known in my lifetime.

"As I began to praise the Lord, the Holy Spirit responded and ministered a miracle to my life. Instead of my lungs closing up with emphysema, the process was reversed. The Lord inhabited my praises. He opened my lungs, and I began to be made whole from that time on. In a few days, I was released from the hospital, made completely whole by the power of the Lord!"

The Word teaches that God "*inhabitest the praises*" of His people (Psalm 22:3 KJV). This man's testimony reminds us that the Lord still inhabits our praises, and miracles result as we lavish loving praises upon Him.

Believe the Lord for Every Healing

Some people find it easy to believe the Lord for healing of arthritis or heart trouble but cannot believe that He will heal a life-threatening illness like cancer.

However, when Christ suffered at Calvary for your sins, it was not for only some of your sins. He "*forgives all your iniquities*" (Psalm 103:3). He forgives adultery and murder as easily as He forgives a "little white lie." By the same token, when He purchased your healing with His stripes, it included cancer just as much as it did arthritis or heart trouble. It is no harder for Him to heal one disease than it is another, for the Lord "*heals all your diseases*" (Psalm 103:3).

The Bible teaches that "*Christ has redeemed us from the curse of the law, having become a curse for us (for it is written, 'Cursed is everyone who hangs on a tree')*" (Galatians 3:13). What was that curse? It is recorded in Deuteronomy 28, where we find listed many diseases that would come upon the people if they disobeyed God's law. Following a lengthy list of all kinds of diseases, the curse included being afflicted "*from the sole of your foot to the top of your head*" (Deuteronomy 28:35).

Christ reversed the curse. In order to redeem us from this terrible curse of the law, He was made a curse; that is, He bore the punishment prescribed by the law. That is why He had to take our infirmities and bear our sicknesses. (See Matthew 8:17.) Since He was made a curse for us, He redeemed us from the curse of the law, providing healing from the tops of our heads to the soles of our feet.

What a thrill to know that God so loved us that He paid a great price for our redemption from sin and *all forms* of sickness!

God's Will and Your Healing

Someone came to me who had been sick for years. As I talked with this person, I said, "If I pray for you now, will you receive your healing?"

He said, "I am not sure that it would be the will of the Lord to heal me." This is a very common difficulty for many devout, honest hearts.

I asked this person, "Are you taking any medicine?"

He said, "Oh yes, I am taking medicine. I am under a doctor's care now."

I said, "What's the object in that?"

He looked at me, confused, and said, "Why, to get well."

I said, "I thought you said that you did not know whether it was the Father's will or not for you to be well. If it is not the Father's will for you to be healed, you are sinning dreadfully in taking medicine and having a doctor. Let the sickness run its limit."

He looked at me.

I said, "I mean every word. If it is not the Father's will for you to be well, you, as a Christian, ought to cut out the medicine."

In many cases, we say that we do not know if it is the Father's will to heal us, and yet we are trying everything we can and everything that anybody else suggests in an effort to be healed. It just proves one thing: you are talking to cover up your lack of faith!

If it is not the Father's will for you to be healed, stop taking medicine. If you don't know whether it is His will or not, it is your business to find out; and you can find out—very easily.

I cannot conceive of it being the Father's will that anyone should be sick. He is not that kind of a Father. When Jesus came, He was the revealed will of the Father, and Jesus healed everybody who came to Him. Jesus did not pick out a case and say, "Now, I think you will have to stay sick. I cannot heal you, because it is not the will of the Father for you." Do you see the point? Jesus was the will of the Father, and He healed everyone.

You might ask, "Why doesn't everyone receive healing?" You might speak of one of Paul's companions who was left behind ill. I can understand that. I can understand Paul's being sick; I can understand any of the disciples being sick.

How? They were just out of the will of the Father for a little bit. They were human, just as we are. If Paul had to leave that man sick, it was because the man was not where Paul's prayers would reach him. I have had this happen continually among those I know.

Paul's Thorn in the Flesh

Another might ask, "What about Paul's thorn in the flesh?" Well, if you read it carefully, it will solve the whole problem.

Paul said in 2 Corinthians 12:7 that because of the greatness of the revelations he had been given, there was given to him a thorn in the flesh, to prevent him from becoming *"exalted above measure."* He described the thorn in the flesh as *"a messenger of Satan"* to buffet him.

He said that he asked the Lord three times to take this demon away, but the Lord said, *"My grace is sufficient for you, for My strength is made perfect in weakness"* (verse 9). Paul said, "Amen, then, I will go on with this problem so that the power of God may rest upon me." (See verses 9–10.)

You can talk about a thorn in the flesh if you have received revelations so great that God thinks it is dangerous lest you become high-minded and conceited, but I do not think there are any of us who have received any revelations from God so great that they endanger our walk with Him. Paul was different. He was let into the inside of things as no other human being ever was, or possibly ever will be, until Jesus comes.

But you might ask, "How is it that so many are sick and have so many people praying for them?" Prayer does not mean anything unless there is faith in it. It is the faith in prayer that makes prayer effectual. You may pray all night for a solid week, but if you do not believe, you will not receive anything.

It is believing that brings results. It is the prayer of faith that shall save the sick—not the prayer of words. It is not the anointing oil but the prayer of faith that shall save the sick, and it is the Lord who will raise them up. (See James 5:14–15.)

You see that the will of the Father is Jesus, and Jesus is the Healer; so, until Jesus stops being the will of the Father, I will believe that healing is mine and is a part of the redemptive work of Christ. For "*by His stripes we are healed*" (Isaiah 53:5).

I stand squarely on that truth. He bore my diseases, my sicknesses, and my infirmities in His body upon that tree. I believe it profoundly and rest there securely in His name.

Must Jesus Bear Our Sins and Diseases Again?

Jesus was made sin for us. God "*made Him who knew no sin to be sin for us*" (2 Corinthians 5:21), and "*surely He has borne our griefs and carried our sorrows*" (Isaiah 53:4).

Have you ever realized that when you ask the Father to heal you today, you are asking Him to do something He has already done in Christ? When you ask someone to pray for your diseases so that you may be healed, have you ever realized that you are repudiating Isaiah 53:4? You are counting it as though it was never written. You are asking Him to do again what He already did for you.

When the intelligent person has done something wrong, he simply asks the Father to forgive him and to cleanse him from that unrighteous act. When the believer is sick, he should remember that sickness is a sin of the body—a sin of the senses. When you grasp this truth, disease and sickness will not be so formidable. You will know that you have been healed and that healing is permanent. If Satan brings disease upon you, all you need to do is confess to God, like this:

> Father, I am sorry that I permitted the adversary to touch my body, the holy temple of God. Now, in Jesus' name, I command the power of the adversary to be broken over it, and I take my perfect deliverance, in Jesus' name. Amen.

Healing is not a problem of faith, as we understand that term, because healing has already taken place, and "*by His stripes we are healed*" (Isaiah 53:5). You will have this realization when you learn that His substitutionary sacrifice is a reality. But as long as you talk sickness and confess sickness, the adversary will take advantage of your confession and make it a reality in your body.

You are afraid of drafts because you believe you are going to catch a cold. I have not had a cold since I learned my place in Christ, learned to take it, and learned to act as though it were true. You do not need to be sick; healing was fully accomplished when Christ rose from the dead, and it belongs to you.

Now, understand this fact: the Father does not say to you, as a child, "Son, if you have faith in Me, I will heal you." Jesus talked like that to those old covenant men when He lived on earth, but when He speaks to you, a son or a daughter, He knows it is not a problem of faith on your part. That healing belongs to you. When you accepted Jesus, you accepted your healing.

So, with quiet confidence, you look up into your Father's face and thank Him for your perfect deliverance.

They Will Recover

D elmar Kingsriter is a missionary to Malawi, Africa, where he has served the Lord for many years. He shared this amazing experience of how we can boldly employ the mighty spiritual weapons the Lord has given us to live in divine health. This is a testimony of bold Bible living across the world.

> *And these signs will follow those who believe:*
> *In My name they will cast out demons; they*
> *will speak with new tongues; they will take*
> *up serpents; and if they drink anything dead-*
> *ly, it will by no means hurt them; they will*
> *lay hands on the sick, and **they will recover**.*
> (Mark 16:17–18, emphasis added)

"Mark 16 certainly must be a favorite Scripture for many missionaries. It certainly is mine, for it provides me both defensive and offensive weapons for divine health. Satan is well aware of the devastating results when the prayer of faith is offered for the sick.

"Since the time of Christ, the healing of the sick has been the most potent weapon in the hands of God's servants. Therefore, Satan often seeks to destroy those who are carrying the message of deliverance from sin and sickness. There have been many occasions when I've had to quote and claim this Scripture because satanic powers were seeking to destroy my very existence.

"I recall one occasion when a missionary family, together with myself, my wife, and my children, traveled by boat to a remote village in Africa. The gospel had first penetrated this village only a few weeks before, and we were seeing wonderful success.

"After a glorious meeting, crowned by a water baptismal service, we had just begun the three-hour journey back to our base camp when a huge swarm of poisonous African bees attacked us. Before we were able to find shelter in a smoke-filled hut, each of us had sustained as many as fifty to seventy-five stings, mostly around the face and head. I realized that we were in danger of losing our lives, for many people have died after being stung only a few times.

"Within moments, the wife of the other missionary became desperately ill and collapsed in the dust. It was in that instant that this Scripture became very precious to me and seemed to be the last thread of hope between life and death. None of us present that day can ever doubt the power of the Word of

God. We gathered around this still form and quietly quoted Mark 16:18. Then, we offered a simple but desperate plea for help to the only One who could help us in that hour—the Lord Jesus Christ.

"Within a few seconds, color came back into the face of that missionary's wife, and she stood up and said, 'I am well.' All the way back to the camp, our little children joined us in worshipping the Lord for a mighty deliverance. There was not a sign on any of us of the swelling that usually accompanied the stings of even the less poisonous honey bee.

"This is a modern-day deliverance, not unlike that of the three Hebrew children whom God delivered from the fiery furnace. Is it any wonder this Scripture verse has become one of my favorites?"

Common Questions about Healing

Most people would agree that health is a universal word. Those who have lost it desire it above everything else. Those who have it employ every means to maintain it.

It is obvious from God's Word that He has a great deal to say about health. My firm conviction is that if we gave more attention to the clear provisions that God makes for healthy bodies through our Lord Jesus Christ, we would be living fuller, more victorious Christian lives than we ever dreamed possible. We would enjoy bold Bible living that would attract the unsaved of the world to our doorsteps to obtain the same thing!

Because there are some very common questions regarding healing that I have received from all over the world, I would like to answer several of them. Perhaps you have asked some of these questions yourself or know a friend who needs these answers. I pray that they will be a blessing to further your bold Bible walk.

"I have received prayer for my healing. What must I do now?"

After you have had prayer for your healing, my challenge to you is to do what the Word says and act on its promises. The Bible promises us that we are healed through Christ (see, for example, Isaiah 53:5), so affirm what God says about your healing. Make it personal and declare, "By His stripes I am healed." Then, begin to thank and praise the Lord for healing you, for praise is the language of faith.

One night, before a Crusade service, I was invited to accompany the pastor of the church where I was ministering on a visit. We went to the home of a man who had been completely bedridden for eighteen months due to a paralytic stroke. Since the message of divine healing was comparatively new to this man, I explained to him the truth of Mark 16:17–18, where Jesus said, *"These signs will follow those who believe:… they will lay hands on the sick, and they will recover."*

I said to the man, "Not everyone for whom we pray is healed instantly. But as surely as you take

142

this verse from Jesus Christ in faith and hold fast to it without wavering, He says you shall recover. It may be instantly, or it may be a matter of hours or days. But this is a positive statement: "You *will* recover!"

This man received the truth with an open mind and heart and assured me of his confidence in Christ's ability to make the Word real in his life. The pastor and I laid hands on him in the name of Jesus and prayed for his healing. Although there were no immediate visible results, this man was not dismayed. He was trustful that the Lord would perform His promise.

We had given him the basis for healing: by Christ's stripes we are healed. He had realized that the *finished work of Christ* gives us provision for healing, but our *faith* must produce the full benefit of it in our lives.

I noticed a large clock just adjacent to the bedroom door that chimed on the hour, and I asked the man to make a bold affirmation of faith every time he heard the hall clock chime that another hour of the day or night had passed. The paralytic man agreed that he would look up every time he heard the clock chime the hour, and he would say, "Thank You, Jesus, for by Your stripes I am healed."

The paralytic stroke had left this man's fingers drawn up, his face and mouth disfigured and turned to one side, and his legs drawn. So it was with real effort that he began to exclaim triumphantly, "Thank You, Jesus, for by Your stripes I am healed." This all happened on a Monday night. I left to go back to my home that same evening.

On Thursday morning, our paralytic friend called his pastor on the phone and said, "Come out, Pastor, I have something wonderful I want to share with you." The pastor went to the home, and there he witnessed a mighty miracle. This same man who had been virtually a prisoner of his bed of suffering stood in the living room smiling and declaring, "It his worked just like Brother Gossett assured me! I have praised in faith, and the Lord has healed me!" The man's fingers were straightened out, his legs were normal, and the disfigurement of the mouth and face were all gone. He was completely healed of the paralytic stroke!

I relate this miraculous account so that you may realize the importance of rising up with a new testimony that harmonizes with the Word of God. Hold fast to that testimony, boldly and without wavering, for God, who has given His Word, will watch over that Word to perform it.

This is a challenge of utmost importance. Begin to confess your healing. Believe it from your heart. See Christ taking on your infirmities and diseases in His own body. Then, realize that through the bleeding stripes He endured, He provided healing for you. Now, repeat from a full heart, "Thank You, Jesus, for by Your stripes I am healed." These are

144

not magic words. They are words that harmonize with God's Word, and God watches over His Word to make it good. It will happen in your behalf!

"I don't feel any different, even though I have been prayed for."

Well, beloved, this is perhaps the greatest pitfall in healing that we ever meet. Feeling is not faith. Your feelings will deceive you. When prayed for according to the Bible, some people do feel differently. But faith in God accepts the healing regardless of feelings, knowing that God cannot lie. (See Numbers 23:19.)

He promised, *"I am the LORD who heals you"* (Exodus 15:26). Whether you feel God's power in your body or not, the whole matter rests with His Word. The Bible says, *"They will lay hands on the sick, and they will recover"* (Mark 16:18), and *"He sent His word and healed them"* (Psalm 107:20). All healing is based on the authority of the Word. Christ healed the sick and cast out evil spirits with His own Word.

There is another remarkable testimony that confirms the power in Mark 16:18. I know of a woman whose doctors had pronounced her incurably ill. She made many attempts to receive her healing, going again and again for prayer. But, after many months, she only grew worse and became discouraged. Then, she heard our *Bold Bible Living* broadcast, and the truth that *"they will lay hands on the sick, and they will recover"* challenged her. She realized that it wasn't in the many prayers of others that she would be healed but by steadfastly believing this promise of Jesus and acting accordingly.

Friends tried to discourage her, even as she maintained her new confession. "How are you feeling?" they would inquire. "You're not looking well at all," they would add, sympathetically.

"I'm not going on how I look or feel," she would answer, refusing to waver in her faith. "Jesus said, *'They will lay hands on the sick, and they will recover,'* and that's for me. I have had hands laid on me for my healing, and I know I am recovering."

These "Job" comforters persisted in trying to throw cold water on her fervent confession, but she was resolute. She had received hands laid upon her body, and she expected the Lord to be faithful. She would not dishonor Him by disbelieving His promises. Her part in this drama of faith was to hold fast to her confession without wavering. (See Hebrews 10:23.)

She fought a good fight of faith. The Lord made her completely whole! Believe His Word. Make it your testimony. Act boldly upon it. And you, too, will know the truth, *"He sent His word and healed them"* (Psalm 107:20).

"I don't seem to have the faith. I guess I won't be healed."

Listen, beloved, if you are a Christian, you do have the faith. "*God has dealt to each one a measure of faith*" (Romans 12:3). Use that faith! Put it into action. You will be made whole. Declare assuredly, "I do have faith. I do believe!"

You ask, "Well, how can I strengthen my faith?" The Bible says that "*faith comes by hearing, and hearing by the word of God*" (Romans 10:17). Study, soak in God's Word. Accept the glorious promises at face value and act boldly accordingly!

"*What if old symptoms of the affliction I had return?*"

Recognize that it is a trick of Satan. "*Resist the devil and he will flee from you*" (James 4:7).

A couple of years ago, I awakened one morning with a splitting headache. The pain was so severe that it seemed like the back of my skull was breaking off from the rest of my head. These pains began to recur almost daily. It was very unusual for me because head pains were something I had never experienced before in my life.

The headaches reached a climax in severity the following month while my wife and I were at a crusade. I determined then that I must meet with the Lord in prayer, praise, and the confession of His Word. The Bible prophesies,

> *It shall come to pass in the last days, says God, that I will pour out of My Spirit on all flesh;*

147

your sons and your daughters shall prophesy,
your young men shall see visions, your old men
shall dream dreams. (Acts 2:17)

In the early morning, as I lay on my bed confessing "by His stripes I am healed," I had an unusual experience. I saw a man come toward me and lay his hand on the back of my head. A warm, penetrating oil flowed into the "split" there and ministered healing, taking away all the pain. To the best of my knowledge, I said, "Sir, you must be the apostle Paul," which was a strange statement to make. But then he replied, "I am an angel of the Lord."

Hebrews 1:14 declares that angels are ministering spirits sent forth to minister to the heirs of salvation. When I returned to a state of complete awareness, all of the pain was gone! I told Joyce about the experience, and, a little later, I shared it with the other ministers at the crusade. Everyone rejoiced with me at the Lord's goodness.

But, unexpectedly, when we returned home the next week, the heavy pains in my head returned. I was somewhat dismayed at the return of the pain, until suddenly, I realized that the headaches were actually lying symptoms and not the real physical pains at all. Jesus had already provided healing; it was His Word that I had confessed when the healing was manifested at the crusade. That night, I had one more bout with the lying symptoms of headaches. I resisted them emphatically in Jesus' conquering name, and the pains left, never to return again!

In John 10:10, Jesus revealed that the devil is a thief who comes *"to steal, and to kill, and to destroy."* The old thief sought to steal the healing the Lord had performed for me. However, realizing the power of God's Word, I refused to accept anything that would destroy the reality of the healing work of Jesus. I praise the Lord. I have not had a headache since—not even for a moment!

You have the right, as a believer, to defeat the devil in the all-powerful name of Jesus. The Bible tells us that we overcome the devil by the blood of Jesus and the word of our testimony. (See Revelation 12:11.) Know the power of the blood. Know the authority of the Word in your testimony. Use them boldly!

A Few Miracles

Let us close this chapter on miracles and healing by studying a few of Jesus' wondrous acts. A miracle is above the sensory realm but in perfect harmony with revelation. It is important to understand these two types of knowledge.

There are two different kinds of knowledge in the world: knowledge that comes to fallen man through the five senses, and knowledge that has come to us through the revelation that is called the Bible. Miracles belong to the revelation kind of knowledge. Reason from the senses has always warred against revelation and against the miracles that revelation has claimed.

You cannot harmonize these two. There is no harmony between them. They belong to two distinct realms. When we try to harmonize what is known as sensory or human reason with revelation, we find many insurmountable obstacles. Let revelation knowledge have its place, and let human reason have its place.

Jesus at Cana

The story of Jesus turning water into wine at the wedding in Cana is one that has challenged reason at every angle.

Had Jesus objected to marriage festivities, He never would have attended. When they found that the amount of wine was inadequate for the festivities, Jesus' mother said to Him, "*They have no wine*" (John 2:3). This is what followed:

> *There were set there six waterpots of stone, according to the manner of purification of the Jews, containing twenty or thirty gallons apiece. Jesus said to them, "Fill the waterpots with water." And they filled them up to the brim. And He said to them, "Draw some out now, and take it to the master of the feast." And they took it. When the master of the feast had tasted the water that was made wine, and did not know where it came from (but the servants who had drawn the water knew), the master of the feast called the bridegroom. And he said to him, "Every man at the beginning sets out the good wine, and when the guests have well drunk, then the inferior. You have kept the good wine until now!"* (John 2:6–10)

Most of what we call "the laws of nature" are laws that came into being when man became the subject of Satan. But when Jesus walked among men, He set aside these laws whenever it was necessary. For example, He caused limbs that had been maimed to become new limbs.

In this miracle, Jesus showed Himself to be absolute Lord and Creator.

The Centurion's Servant

One of the great laws of Jesus' ministry is unveiled to us in the story of the healing of the centurion's servant. In Matthew 8:7, Jesus said, "I will come and heal him."

> *The centurion answered and said, "Lord, I am not worthy that You should come under my roof. But only speak a word, and my servant will be healed.* [Here was a man who knew the power of words!] *For I also am a man under authority, having soldiers under me. And I say to this one, 'Go,' and he goes; and to another, 'Come,' and he comes.* (Matthew 8:8–9)

In other words, he said, "Master, diseases are Your servants. All You need to do is to speak the word, and that disease will depart." Jesus said, "*I have not found such great faith, not even in Israel!*" (verse 10). Then, turning to the centurion, He said, "*Go your way; and as you have believed, so let it be done for you*" (verse 13). And the man's servant was healed that very hour.

Now, we come face-to-face with the centurion's faith in the words of Christ. That centurion knew that the moment Jesus spoke, his servant would be healed. I wish that all who read this would have as much confidence in God's Word as that Gentile centurion.

Verse 16 goes on to tell us, "*They brought to Him many who were demon-possessed. And He cast out the spirits with a word, and healed all who were sick.*" Every healing, every demon cast out, and every other miracle that the Master performed were performed through His Word.

In Genesis 1, God spoke and said, "*Let there be light*" (verse 3). He said, "*Let the waters under the heavens be gathered together into one place, and let the dry land appear*" (verse 9). Then, He said to the water, "Be filled with life." (See verse 20.) He said to the land, "Give forth vegetation." (See verse 11.)

That is the Word with which we are dealing. By the Word of God, the universe was brought into being. By the Word of God, you are born again, made a new creation. By the Word of God, you are healed from every disease. By the Word of God, we are more than conquerors in every way.

The Feeding of the Five Thousand

The feeding of the five thousand is one of the most interesting as well as illuminating miracles of the Master. It reveals to us some features about the

Master's ministry and about the life of faith that we find in no other place.

Jesus and His disciples were in a desert place. Jesus had gone apart to be alone. The multitudes followed Him.

> *When Jesus went out He saw a great multitude; and He was moved with compassion for them, and healed their sick. When it was evening, His disciples came to Him, saying, "This is a deserted place, and the hour is already late. Send the multitudes away, that they may go into the villages and buy themselves food." But Jesus said to them, "They do not need to go away. You give them something to eat." And they said to Him, "We have here only five loaves and two fish." He said, "Bring them here to Me." Then He commanded the multitudes to sit down on the grass. And He took the five loaves and the two fish, and looking up to heaven, He blessed and broke and gave the loaves to the disciples.*
> (Matthew 14:14–19)

And it multiplied in His hands until that vast company of five thousand had been fed, and they took up twelve baskets full of leftovers. (See verses 20–21.)

What an expression of love, of miraculous grace, is unveiled here! This miracle was not to display Jesus' ability only, for Jesus also said, "*Whatever you ask in My name, that I will do*" (John 14:13). He is

154

under His own obligation to give us bread if we ask for it. Hunger is unnecessary if we walk with Him.

If Jesus could take five little loaves and two fishes, ask the Father's blessing upon them, and have them multiply to feed five thousand men, then He meant that you could do the same. You can take your limited food and ask the blessing on it, and it will meet every need. You can take those four or five dollars and make them multiply until you can pay your bills. A little, when blessed by the Lord, becomes much.

"Lazarus, Come Forth!"

Of all the stories of the miracles performed by the Master, none has had greater influence than the raising of Lazarus from the dead. You can approach it from any angle, and it becomes a loudspeaker filled with grace and helpfulness.

Lazarus had been dead for four days when Jesus came to the home of his sisters, Martha and Mary. When Martha went out to meet Him, she cried, *"Lord, if You had been here, my brother would not have died"* (John 11:21).

> *Jesus said to her, "Your brother will rise again." Martha said to Him, "I know that he will rise again in the resurrection at the last day." Jesus said to her, "I am the resurrection and the life. He who believes in Me, though he may die, he shall live. And whoever lives and believes in*

155

Me shall never die. Do you believe this?" She
said to Him, "Yes, Lord, I believe that You are
the Christ, the Son of God, who is to come into
the world."   (John 11:23–27)

Martha was not a believer in the true sense. She
was a mental assenter. She is the most graphic illustration of this. But when Mary came, she uttered
the same statement, *"Lord, if You had been here, my*
brother would not have died" (verse 32).

> [Jesus] *said, "Where have you laid him?"*
> *They said to Him, "Lord, come and see."…*
> *Jesus said, "Take away the stone." Mar-*
> *tha, the sister of him who was dead, said to*
> *Him, "Lord, by this time there is a stench,*
> *for he has been dead four days." Jesus said to*
> *her, "Did I not say to you that if you would*
> *believe you would see the glory of God?"*
> (John 11:34, 39–40)

Martha had not believed. She had been so occupied by worldly things that real faith had not entered her heart. I can see Mary standing with open
hands, waiting for the next command of the Master.
Then, "[Jesus] *cried with a loud voice, 'Lazarus,*
come forth!' And he who had died came out bound
hand and foot with graveclothes, and his face was
wrapped with a cloth" (verses 43–44).

Oh, the fearlessness of that Man. In the face of a
decaying body, He dared to risk His reputation and
shouted, *"Lazarus, come forth!"* Again, the words

of the Master are the words of God, and they have creative energy in them.

"If Only I May Touch His Clothes..."

For our last notable miracle, we return to the story recorded in Mark 5:25–34 of the woman with the issue of blood, who had spent all her money on physicians and was not healed by any of them. But she said within her heart, *"If only I may touch His clothes, I shall be made well"* (verse 28).

Someone had told this weak woman about the Master. One look into His face had been enough. She heard those gracious words fall from His lips, and now she crawled through the crowd, a broken thing, so weak her limbs would not sustain her. She reached her hand through and touched the hem of His garment, and she felt in her body that she was healed.

Remember her confession: *"If only I may touch His clothes, I shall be made well."* There was no doubt or fear there. It was faith daring to reach forth and touch the hem of His garment. She did not ask for His hand to touch her. She asked for nothing but the opportunity of touching His garment.

No sooner had she touched Him than Jesus said, *"'Who touched My clothes?' But His disciples said to Him, 'You see the multitude thronging You'"* (Mark 5:30–31). "Oh, no," Jesus said, "It was not that kind of a touch. It was a faith touch." (See Luke 8:46.)

He can be touched today with the feeling of our infirmities. He, the One who was tempted in all points, can be touched now by you, and He knows when your faith reaches out and touches Him. (See Hebrews 4:14–16.)

He demanded faith then. His work was not finished then; He was just the Healer of Israel. But now, His work is finished, and He is seated at the right hand of God in the heavenlies; by the stripes He bore, healing is yours today.

All that He did is yours *now*. Take Him as your Savior and enter into all that He purchased for you.

Overcoming Fear
and Difficulty

Fear Has No Part in My Heart

Herbert Hoover, thirty-first president of the United States, once said upon returning home from a world tour, "The dominant emotion everywhere is fear. This applies to every part of human activity: finances, industry, farmers, workers, thinkers, and government officials."

That was a strong statement from a highly esteemed man, and it is a fact that sadly still holds true today. When I consider the amazing number of people in all walks of life who are obsessed by some inward fear, I feel the responsibility as a servant of God to declare that you *can* be free from fear!

What Is Fear?

Just what is fear? Fear has been defined as the expectation or apprehension of evil.

Within limits, fear can be a good thing. We cannot live either our natural or our spiritual lives without it. A child will burn himself unless he has a proper fear of fire. A pedestrian will be knocked down and perhaps killed unless he has a respectful fear of traffic. A man cannot be a successful Christian unless he respectfully fears God, for "*the fear of the LORD is the beginning of knowledge*" (Proverbs 1:7). It is healthy to fear both danger and sin.

But there's another kind of fear that is very unhealthy. This is the fear that brings torment. (See 1 John 4:18.) It is the fear that causes you to always expect the bad. This fear is an insidious monster that, if it takes its full course in your life, will produce misery, defeat, bondage, and destruction.

Fear creates nervous breakdowns, sleeplessness, oppression in your prayer life, and bondage in witnessing. Fear can lead to an urge to commit suicide. It can be manifested in stinginess toward God in your giving. Fear can truly be defined as the expectation of bad things.

Satan wants you to have this diabolical spirit of fear, which expects and magnifies evil, failure, sickness, danger, and worry. I realize the tremendous significance of a statement made by Dr. Len Jones of Australia: "Fear is the devil's second name!"

Many people do not recognize fear when it poses as prudence, caution, or discretion. But we must come to grips with this and realize that these really may be fears disguised by the devil. Satan will use every subtle device he can find to hinder the good things of God. I believe that fear is the greatest spiritual hindrance keeping people from completely yielding themselves to God and enjoying a rich, abundant life in Jesus Christ.

I challenge you! Do not knuckle under to fear. Resist fear and you will overcome. *"Resist the devil and he will flee from you"* (James 4:7). Affirm this with me: "Fear has no part in my heart!"

Overcoming Fear

I have had many interesting discussions with a prominent psychiatrist from Washington, D.C., whom I met overseas. We share a concern for the vast number of people whose lives are shrouded in fear. Because the giant called Fear is slaying thousands, it is important that Christians embrace God's truth: *"For God has not given us a spirit of fear, but of power and of love and of a sound mind"* (2 Timothy 1:7). As we look to the promises in God's Word, we can possess full assurance that we can live free from fear, for fear has no part in the heart of a redeemed child of God.

One such Scripture says, *"Fear not, for I am with you; be not dismayed, for I am your God. I will strengthen you, yes, I will help you, I will uphold you with My righteous right hand"* (Isaiah 41:10).

As long as God is with you, fear need have no part in your heart. He has promised, *"I am with you always, even to the end of the age"* (Matthew 28:20).

God's Word says, *"Fear not, for I have redeemed you; I have called you by your name; you are Mine"* (Isaiah 43:1). Because the Lord has redeemed you, you are delivered from the power of Satan, the author of fear.

"The LORD is on my side; I will not fear. What can man do to me?" (Psalm 118:6). *"The fear of man brings a snare, but whoever trusts in the LORD shall be safe"* (Proverbs 29:25). You need not be snared again by a spirit that fears man. Because the Lord is with you, man can do nothing to you. *"That we, being delivered from the hand of our enemies, might serve Him without fear, in holiness and righteousness before Him all the days of our life"* (Luke 1:74–75).

Because God is your unfailing Helper, you can boldly say, "Fear has no part in my heart!" (See Hebrews 13:5–6; Deuteronomy 31:6; 2 Chronicles 32:7–8; Psalm 3:6–7; 27:1–3.)

Like Joshua, you can stand fearlessly in the presence of gigantic foes. Like David, you can come against the giants in your life in the all-conquering name of the Lord. You can be free from fear as God gives you courage, confidence, fearlessness, and the daring to do what His Word declares you can do.

God Will Deliver You

Y*ou called in trouble, and I delivered you"* (Psalm 81:7). This sounds like our own personal experience—a leaf out of our own history. We called and He heard us.

In a recent meeting, I asked for a show of hands of those who had received answers to prayers since the previous meeting. With faces aglow, hands uplifted, and voices filled with praise, people told of answered prayers. They had called in their troubles, and He had answered in faithfulness.

We came with our burdens and heartaches, and He took them. We came with our cares, and He assumed them. We came with our diseases, and He healed them.

Our hearts are filled with praise and worship and adoration because we know that the God of the universe is our own Father. He loves us.

If He carried Israel in His bosom (see Isaiah 40:11), He carries us in His heart. If He engraved them upon the palms of His hands (see Isaiah 49:16), He has us hidden away in Christ (see Colossians 3:3). Oh, the wealth of the riches of His glory and love!

We called, and He has answered. The Master said, "*Whatever you ask in My name, that I will do*" (John 14:13). Note that He said, "*I will do.*" You ask, you pray, you intercede, and He will answer, He will do, He will work.

"Fear Not, for I Am with You"

Isaiah 41:10 stands as the challenge of the ages: "*Fear not, for I am with you; be not dismayed, for I am your God. I will strengthen you, yes, I will help you, I will uphold you with My righteous right hand.*" This is the challenge of love. This is God talking to your heart.

There is no place for weakness and no place for fear. This is the basis for success. Failure cannot abide here. Jesus said, "*I am with you always*" (Matthew 28:20). This is partnership. This is companionship.

When He said, "*I am the vine, you are the branches*" (John 15:5), He meant that this is the place from which you draw your strength. You cannot be weak with Him as your strength.

Self-depreciation, which we have been calling humility, is of the devil. God never made a weak man; God never made a failure. When

He became the strength of your life, you were strong. (See Psalm 27:1.) You may not have used His strength; you may not have known it, but you have had the ability of God in you. You are already an overcomer.

God will whisper to your heart that you are an overcomer. When He whispers to your heart Romans 8:31, "*If God is for us, who can be against us?*" you had better rise up and go into the fight! You can conquer in anything He calls you to.

"Nothing Will Be Impossible for You"

Right now, we are standing in the presence of omnipotence. We are standing where God and humanity touch. We are now where man is to take on the strength of God as God took on the weakness of man.

Here, we are laboring together with Christ. He is sharing our burdens; we are sharing His strength. He came to our level to lift us to His own, and He has done it. We are now so utterly united with Him, so much a part of Him, that Paul could say, "*It is no longer I who live, but Christ lives in me*" (Galatians 2:20).

It is not a problem of faith but a problem of understanding our privilege. Jesus has given us the legal right to the use of His name, and Jesus has all the authority in heaven and on earth. Now, we have the power of attorney to use His name.

"*Whatever you ask in My name, that I will do, that the Father may be glorified in the Son*" (John 14:13). Jesus desires that the Father be glorified in Himself, and so He challenges us to use His name.

This is the miracle-name, the wonder-name of Jesus. Can't you see the limitlessness of this life with Him? Can't you see that He meant exactly what He said? "*If two of you agree on earth concerning anything that they ask, it will be done for them by My Father in heaven*" (Matthew 18:19). Prayer becomes a cooperation with Deity. It is not begging or soliciting. It is fellowship. It is carrying out the Father's will.

We have taken the place of Jesus on earth to evangelize the world and to make the church see its wonderful privileges in Christ. Can't you see our ministry? Can't you feel the throb of the heart of God as you read this?

Surely you can see why nothing is impossible to you. That financial problem is not as large as it was, that disease not as formidable, and that trouble not as unconquerable! Listen, and you will hear Him whispering, "*Fear not, for I am with you*" (Isaiah 41:10).

"You Mighty Man of Valor!"

Israel had been reduced to absolute poverty and servitude by enemies. God called on a young man named Gideon, and the story is recorded in Judges 6:12: "*The Angel of the LORD appeared to him, and said to him, 'The LORD is with you, you mighty man of valor!'"*

Then Gideon did the normal thing. He began to talk about how weak and inefficient he was. Somehow or other, that has been the stock and trade through the ages. The ministry plays upon it; the evangelist uses it as a club.

> *The LORD turned to him and said, "Go in this might of yours, and you shall save Israel from the hand of the Midianites. Have I not sent you?" So he said to Him, "O my LORD, how can I save Israel?"* (Judges 6:14–15)

Learn to see yourself through God's eyes. See yourself as God has pictured you in the Word. You are "*born from above*"; you are born of God. (See John 3:3–8.) "*Whatever is born of God overcomes the world*" (1 John 5:4). You are an overcomer.

You may not know it, you may have lived in the realm of sensory knowledge all your life, but God is coming to you today, saying, "*You mighty man of valor!*"

Colossians 2:10 declares that "*you are complete in Him.*" You have received of His fullness, and grace has been poured upon you on top of grace. (See John 1:16.) At this hour, you are more than a conqueror through Him who has loved you. (See Romans 8:37.) Be done with weakness. Be done with self-depreciation. Praise God for what He is in you.

Protection by Day and Night

The very spirit of this age is one of tension, and with the crises in world affairs constantly intensifying, we are reminded that Jesus said, "*Men's hearts* [will fail] *them from fear and the expectation of those things which are coming on the earth*" (Luke 21:26).

I have found that one thing people greatly fear is physical harm, whether it is from catastrophic events, other people, or even some animals. But Christians can rest in God's Word in the face of all sorts of threats against their well-being.

I would like to challenge you now with the following stories from some of our friends in the ministry. Stand strong against fear, for God is your Protector!

The Fear of War

One woman who fought fear with prayer and the Word of God was Mrs. Mabel Chapman of Burnaby, British Columbia. Mrs. Chapman was born and raised in Great Britain, then moved to

Saskatchewan, Canada, where she and her husband and their two sons lived for many years.

When World War II came, Mrs. Chapman's sons entered the Canadian armed services. Soon, they were shipped off to Europe to be a part of some of the most intense battles of the European theatre. Often, as she would hear news reports of the deaths of thousands of soldiers, Mrs. Chapman found every reason to be fearful and anxious.

However, along with a dear prayer partner, Mrs. Chapman decided to take a stand against fear for the safe homecoming of her boys. The two women took bold steps of faith in proclaiming specific Scriptures for her sons that God would protect them and bring them back to her. Included was Psalm 27:3: *"Though an army may encamp against me, my heart shall not fear; though war should rise against me, in this I will be confident."* As a result of her times of fervent prayer, the Holy Spirit gave Mabel Chapman a clear promise that her sons would come back home.

Four years went by, and she didn't see the faces of her sons. When World War II was over, one son came home quickly. She was still confident that the other one would be home. When it was announced that the last troop train was coming to her town, Mrs. Chapman was there with hundreds of other residents to welcome home the final soldiers. She has often described to me her great anticipation as she continued to confess God's promise that both her sons would be home. When the train pulled into the station, the band struck up a hearty welcome to the soldiers. When they marched into the large train station where the townspeople were waiting, leading the entire procession was Mrs. Chapman's oldest son! God had answered this mother's confident prayers. Both her sons came home.

Mabel Chapman is a Christian who stands firmly against the fear Satan tries to bring into our lives.

The Fear of Travel

A friend recently wrote to me with the following words: "I am scheduled to fly to visit my relatives in the East very soon. Frankly, I am not at all excited about it, because I have a dreadful fear of the prospect of flying in an airplane. I know that you have done a good deal of flying and traveling, and I'd like to have some words of encouragement from you to overcome this spirit of fear."

By believing in God's Word, we can possess safety in travel. Many years ago, this truth of God became very precious to me: "*Safety is of the LORD*" (Proverbs 21:31 KJV). When you really believe this Bible promise that safety is of the Lord, you will have no spirit of fear; you will possess confidence.

Again, the Bible says in Psalm 33:17, "*A horse is a vain hope for safety.*" It can be paraphrased for today that a car is a vain hope for safety, or an airplane is a vain hope for safety. Even your home is a vain hope for safety. Your safety is not in the locks on the door or in the seat belts in the car or plane, but your safety is truly in the Lord. The Lord wants us to exercise wisdom and take proper precautionary measures to protect ourselves, but real safety is in Him.

Begin to confess that the Lord is your Protector against being in a plane accident. Confess that the eyes of the Lord are upon you wherever you go. (See Psalm 33:18–19.) Confess that you do not need to fear because God will take care of you. Confess that God is protecting you, whether you are at home or on an airplane. Here's a wonderful Scripture whereby God assures us of safety, both by day and by night:

> *You will walk safely in your way, and your foot will not stumble. When you lie down, you will not be afraid; yes, you will lie down and your sleep will be sweet. Do not be afraid of sudden terror, nor of trouble from the wicked when it comes; for the LORD will be your confidence, and will keep your foot from being caught.*
> (Proverbs 3:23–26)

You can put your name into each verse here in Proverbs 3 and confess it as yours: that you shall be kept safely, that your foot will not stumble, and that you can praise the Lord.

"Whoever listens to me will dwell safely, and will be secure, without fear of evil" (Proverbs 1:33). Here God promises you that as you listen to Him, You will dwell safely.

Of course, our ultimate safety is in the name of the Lord. Remember Proverbs 18:10: *"The name of the LORD is a strong tower; the righteous run to it and are safe."* Our safety is in the precious, wonderful name of our Lord Jesus Christ. Have great confidence in His name!

The Fear of Nature

The elements of nature can, at times, be frightening to people and cause not only undesirable results but also the continual harassment of fear. Mr. Arthur Thomas of Alberta, Canada, wrote to me about overcoming this particular type of fear.

"I have a testimony of overcoming fear that I've never shared before, but it will interest you because it shows how standing on God's Word can be so effective. We've had an abnormal number of wasps in this area during the summer months for the past few years. Until three years ago, a wasp sting never gave me much concern other than the initial burning sensation, which soon passed away.

"Three years ago, however, in midsummer, I received a sting, and several minutes later, the surrounding scenery became wavy and everything seemed to look yellow. Added to this was extreme difficulty in breathing, along with a horrible taste in my mouth. I ended up collapsing on the ground for about five minutes. Eventually, I gained strength and got to my home. There, I was overtaken with extreme chills so that I had to take a hot bath. Within an hour, things were back to normal.

"The same thing happened the following summer and then again last summer. By this time, I had developed a real fear of wasps and was living in daily dread of being stung again. Several friends had suggested getting shots as an antidote or else carrying pills to take when I was stung again. Somehow, I didn't feel like this was the answer, and, as a result, the Lord showed me the following Scriptures."

He shall deliver you in six troubles, yes, in seven no evil shall touch you. In famine He shall redeem you from death, and in war from the power of the sword. You shall be hidden from the scourge of the tongue, and you shall not be afraid of destruction when it comes. You shall laugh at destruction and famine, and you shall not be afraid of the beasts of the earth. For you shall have a covenant with the stones of the field, and the beasts of the field shall be at peace with you. (Job 5:19–23)

What is man that You are mindful of him, and the son of man that You visit him? For You have made him a little lower than the angels, and You have crowned him with glory and honor. You have made him to have dominion over the works of Your hands; You have put all things under his feet, all sheep and oxen; even the beasts of the field, the birds of the air, and the fish of the sea that pass through the paths of the seas. O LORD, our Lord, how excellent is Your name in all the earth! (Psalm 8:4–9)

Mr. Thomas continued, "Quite often, knowing Scripture and putting it into practice are two different things. Being hearers of the Word is one thing, but also we are commanded to be doers. The Lord kept impressing upon me the importance of claiming these promises, and I did so. Yet, I could still feel my flesh crawl and I would cringe when any of these little creatures came close. I was still fearful.

"This went on for several days until, one day, I accidentally bumped a wasp nest with my head. Wasps don't appreciate this type of familiarity, and immediately they were all around and bouncing off my bare head and face. I know the Lord arranged this, for it forced me to face my fears with His courage. I immediately claimed my authority over the wasps in the name of Jesus, and I never received a sting. Praise God! My fear left. Faith is built by the Word of God, and when we act upon it, then fear has to go."

God's Promises for Protection

In the years that I have been saved, I have had the immeasurable joy of claiming God's promises for protection. I want to share some of those promises with you.

- *"Behold, I am with you and will keep you wherever you go"* (Genesis 28:15).
- *"I will both lie down in peace, and sleep; for You alone, O LORD, make me dwell in safety"* (Psalm 4:8).
- *"Whoever listens to me will dwell safely, and will be secure, without fear of evil"* (Proverbs 1:33).
- *"The LORD is my light and my salvation; whom shall I fear? The LORD is the strength of my life; of whom shall I be afraid?"* (Psalm 27:1).
- *"The beloved of the LORD shall dwell in safety by Him, who shelters him all the day long"* (Deuteronomy 33:12).
- *"He shall give His angels charge over you, to keep you in all your ways"* (Psalm 91:11).
- *"I will say of the LORD, 'He is my refuge and my fortress; my God, in Him I will trust'"* (Psalm 91:2).
- *"The name of the LORD is a strong tower; the righteous run to it and are safe"* (Proverbs 18:10).
- *"For I know whom I have believed and am persuaded that He is able to keep what I have committed to Him until that Day"* (2 Timothy 1:12).
- *"Though I walk in the midst of trouble, You will revive me; You will stretch out Your hand against the wrath of my enemies, and Your right hand will save me"* (Psalm 138:7).

- *"I will put you in the cleft of the rock, and will cover you with My hand"* (Exodus 33:22).

- *"He who dwells in the secret place of the Most High shall abide under the shadow of the Almighty"* (Psalm 91:1).

- *"Who is he who will harm you if you become followers of what is good?"* (1 Peter 3:13).

- *"As the mountains surround Jerusalem, so the LORD surrounds His people from this time forth and forever"* (Psalm 125:2).

- *"The angel of the LORD encamps all around those who fear Him, and delivers them"* (Psalm 34:7).

- *"Many are the afflictions of the righteous, but the LORD delivers him out of them all"* (Psalm 34:19).

You can rejoice that the Lord fills you with strength and protects you wherever you go. (See Psalm 18:32.)

Jesus Had No Sense of Limitations

The world has recognized that Jesus was in a class by Himself. His worst enemies have paid tribute to the fact that He was humanity's loftiest product. Those who do not believe in His incarnation recognize a godlikeness that baffles them.

Jesus had no sense of inferiority in the presence of God. He met the Father God on terms of absolute equality. He spoke of Him as a son speaks of the father with whom he has been in business association for years.

No Sense of Sin

Jesus had no sense of sin. This placed Him in a class by Himself. He never needed forgiveness. He never grieved over His past. He had none of the sense of limitation that comes through sin-consciousness. This alone lifted Him out of the realm in which He moved.

All men have the sense of limitation. They can do only so much. They can endure only so much.

They can live only so long. Man is as conscious of his limitations as a person living on a tiny island in the midst of a vast ocean knows he can go only so far before he reaches his limit.

Jesus had no such consciousness. He knew men. It was not necessary that anyone tell Him anything about Himself or about others. (See John 2:24–25.)

No Fear of Satan

Jesus had no fear of Satan. The fear of Satan is the basis of the sensory-knowledge religions. Man has feared Satan from time immemorial. That fear has kept him in bondage, robbed him of joy, and filled him with anxiety. Man's struggle for freedom has been a struggle against his fear of Satan.

No Fear of Natural Laws

Jesus had no fear of natural laws. All men have lived in conscious dread of certain laws of nature. Jesus did not fear a storm at sea. He did not fear the law of matter conservation. He paid no tribute to either.

Food came when it was needed. Jesus quietly told Peter, *"Launch out into the deep and let down your nets for a catch"* (Luke 5:4). Peter replied, *"Master, we have toiled all night and caught nothing"* (verse 5). Yet, when they let down the net, *"They caught a great number of fish, and their net was breaking"* (verse 6).

In the midst of a desert place with five thousand people, Jesus said to the disciples, *"You give them something to eat*" (Matthew 14:16), as simply as a husband might say to his wife, "Go make a sandwich for this hungry man," knowing that the pantry is full.

Jesus had no fear of lack. Money came when needed. He never paid taxes out of fear, lack, or need. When He and Peter needed to pay their tax, He simply said, in effect, "Go down to the sea and catch a fish; open its mouth, and you will find our money." (See Matthew 17:27.) That was a most unusual thing. But He showed His utter independence from the laws that govern sensory knowledge. Who would dream of finding a piece of silver in a fish's mouth, and who would have the presumption to say, "Go and catch a fish, and the fish you catch will have our tax money in its mouth"?

He was not afraid of God, as other men were. He had an intimate relationship with the Creator of the universe that amazes us. He had no sense of the need of righteousness, the ability to stand in God's presence without fear, guilt, or inferiority. He walked into the presence of the Father as calmly and quietly as I go into the office in the morning.

No Fear of Time

All men are time-conscious. As they begin to draw near to the ends of their lives, they become more conscious of time's limitation. Jesus had no fear of the future. There was a sense of surety in all that He did and said that thrills us.

Jesus had the greatest work of any human being on His hands. His moments meant more than the

180

moments of any other man, yet He had no time-consciousness. He was never in a hurry. He never worried, never fretted, and never spoke unadvisedly. No other man who ever lived had so much depending upon him, so much responsibility, but Christ bore it unconsciously. He faced the cross and its awful consequences with a quietness that staggers us.

He seemed to belong to humanity, yet He was utterly separate from it. He belonged to eternity, yet He lived in time. He belonged in heaven, yet He was perfectly at home among men.

No Sense of Need

All men are subject to the sense of lack and of need. What Christ needed was there, ready for use. All He needed to feed five thousand was five loaves and two fishes. No other man ever dared to talk as Jesus talked or ever dared to presume upon the unseen as He did.

He had no sense of the need for wisdom. He always said the right thing in the right place. He never seemed to reflect. He never reasoned. He never made a mistake. He chose twelve men, and each one of them fitted into His program perfectly. No general ever had such wisdom. No man ever had such insight into character.

No one needed to tell Him anything. He already knew. He had no sense of the need for protection. He did not needlessly put Himself in the way of men's hatred, jealousy, and schemes to arrest Him. He knew the thoughts of men.

No Fear of Disease or Men

All men shrink from contagious diseases, but Christ laid His hand upon the lepers and the ones filled with fever and disease.

He had no consciousness of fear. He never had hatred. Armies are raised and maintained because of the fear of man. We build strong houses and lock them securely because we fear men. We copyright our ideas and patent our inventions because we fear that men will steal them from us.

Our Lord was the absolute Master of men because of His lack of a sense of fear, inferiority, and sin-consciousness.

The Reason Why

Fear of man, fear of certain laws of nature, fear of disease, fear of Satan, and fear of circumstances all come through sin-consciousness. If you take away sin-consciousness from a man, he is utterly fearless.

Jesus met sin as its Conqueror. He met disease as its Master. He met lack and need with a smile because He dominated them. Why? Because He had no sense of sin and no sense of inferiority before God, man, Satan, or anything that Satan could do.

This Man is all that I would expect God to be. I could not ask for God to be different from Jesus. He had perfect wisdom. He had perfect peace. He had perfect self-control. He had perfect dominion over the laws of nature. He read the heart of man as an open book. He stood absolutely alone, a Master, and yet He was utterly one with humanity. He sympathized with their weaknesses. (See Hebrews 4:15.) He felt their limitations, He met their perplexities, and He answered every cry and need of the human.

He could be approached. He was utterly holy, and yet the prostitute and the drunkard and the murderer felt perfectly free in His presence. He was perfectly just, and yet the criminal had no sense of fear. He hated disease and sickness, and yet the multitudes gathered about Him, seeking to touch the hem of His garment and find healing. He had no sense of limitation as He faced human needs.

Fear Creates Disaster in Your Home

I t is crucial that we never give in to the fear that produces in kind in our homes or family lives. Fear produces bondage, and bondage is always the result of Satan's workings. Consequently, fear always activates Satan. It causes him to get busy bringing about the destruction and disaster that you fear. I have seen what fear can activate in my own family life.

Do Not Fear a Disaster in Your Home

In 1957, my wife and I purchased our first home. I was traveling to do evangelistic work, and it was always a struggle to pay the mortgage as well as support my wife and five children. A battle began in the realm of the spirit. I began to fear that I would not be able to make those monthly mortgage payments. Each time I would turn down the road where my family lived, an overwhelming fear would grip me that we would soon lose the home.

Fear activated Satan. As with Job, "*the thing I greatly feared* [came] *upon me, and what I dreaded…*

happened to me" (Job 3:25). I reaped the results of my fears. We moved elsewhere to do the Lord's work. A friend put our house up for rent, but the woman who rented it refused to pay the rent. A sheriff's order was acquired to try to evict her. The woman was extremely clever and was always gone when the sheriff's deputies came to deliver the eviction notice. We had no extra money to pay our house payment plus rent in the new city where we were living.

Satan must have had a gleeful time causing this woman to avoid paying the rent and causing us to have to return our home to the builder. It was a heartbreaking loss.

Then, in 1961, the Holy Spirit visited me in a life-changing way. One of the affirmations He gave me was, "Never again will we confess fear, '*for God has not given us a spirit of fear, but of power and of love and of a sound mind*' (2 Timothy 1:7)."

With this new discipline, my wife and I began to take bold steps of faith. We filed an application to purchase another home. It was another battleground for me the day we signed the papers. Satan attempted to bring back the old tormenting fears that had beset me when we purchased our first home.

I knew that if I gave place to fear, I would activate Satan to do his work of theft again. Jesus revealed Satan's sinister nature in John 10:10: "*The thief does not come except to steal, and to kill, and to destroy. I have come that they may have life, and that they may have it more abundantly.*" When you give place to fear, you give place to the elements of Satan that are designed for destruction, theft, and death.

I praise the Lord that after purchasing our home in 1961, we never missed a single payment, nor were we ever late. As I write these lines, that home is paid for. Satan had no opportunity to steal it from us, for I steadfastly refused to give place to fear.

Do Not Fear a Disaster in Your Marriage

My wife and I have just celebrated thirty years of married life together. I have talked with many people who are married and to many whose marriages have failed. I have endeavored to discover the ingredients that make a marriage last and why marriages crumble. I am convinced that God wants us to experience abundant life in our marriages. This is far more than simply existing together in a bad arrangement.

Most marriages are severely tested. Husbands and wives experience misunderstandings, suffering, pain, and temptation, yet they can rise above all of these things and enjoy great lives together. Good advice for marriage is this: *Don't put off until next year, or ten years from now, the time to begin enjoying your marriage. Don't postpone working for a positive and constructive marriage until things are "ideal."*

One man said, "I thought that when I got out of my deep debts and the children were raised, our marriage would be happy. Now my debts are reduced and the children are all grown, but my wife and I still aren't happy." Another man said, "My wife and I looked forward to our retirement, the time when we would be able to enjoy each other more. But this has not been so. I realize that we let life pass us by and failed to enjoy living together as we went along."

Many are constantly waiting for some future utopia when things will be better. But God's plan is for us to live now, for today, not for an uncertain tomorrow. The Bible says, *"A merry heart does good, like medicine, but a broken spirit dries the bones"* (Proverbs 17:22). Allow a merry heart to exist in your marriage. *"The joy of the LORD is your strength"* (Nehemiah 8:10). Surely, a joyful marriage should abound with the joy of the Lord, not just earthly happiness.

Like a personal Christian walk, marriages become weak and vulnerable to all kinds of problems and defeats *when they lose their joy*. My wife and I enjoy getting away alone at times, but those experiences are the exception, not the rule. It's the day by day dwelling together joyfully that counts! In any marriage, there will be problems: sickness, unexpected trouble, financial difficulties, and confusion. But life goes on regardless, and it's a shame when couples don't enjoy it together.

There was a time when I sadly observed the breakdown of a marriage that was close to me. It began when the husband started confiding in another woman about his problems. This lady was eager to

187

console my friend. It seemed innocent enough at the start, but it opened the door to adultery.

No spouse should tell his or her marriage troubles to someone of the opposite sex who suddenly fills the role of intimate friend. Even if the Lord leads you to marriage counseling, it should be as husband and wife or with your spouse's permission.

We are commanded, *"Trust in the LORD with all your heart, and lean not on your own understanding; in all your ways acknowledge Him, and He shall direct your paths"* (Proverbs 3:5–6). We must lean on Jesus Christ in our times of testing—even in marriage problems. Blessed are the husbands and wives who learn not only to be marriage partners but also true friends! Even though your marriage may have its share of pressures and intense disagreements, it doesn't mean that divorce is a solution.

A lovely young wife whose divorce was to be finalized within a week confessed, "I wish now that I had never used the word *divorce.* We had been married only five years, but we argued so often. Things got pretty bad, and one day I blurted out, 'I think we ought to get a divorce.' We were both shocked at first. We had never even thought of divorce before that moment, but after the shock wore off, I realized that the seed had been planted. It was easier to say the next time. Within weeks, it was all we talked about. The seed grew monstrous roots and finally strangled our marriage."

Others who have been divorced say the same thing. "Tell everybody you can," they say, "to never even speak the word *divorce*. There is something fatal in the very use of the word." They began to talk divorce long before it became a reality. The Bible says, *"Death and life are in the power of the tongue, and those who love it will eat its fruit"* (Proverbs 18:21). There are certain words we must never utter as Bible-believing Christians. Divorce is one of those words we must never employ.

What you say is what you get. Unfortunately, this works for the bad as well as the good. Also, what you fear is what you get. Fear a divorce, and you could be writing your own ticket for a divorce.

The book of Proverbs is a powerful commentary on the power of words. A study of this book not only reveals the ability of right words to conquer life's problems, but it also illuminates the destructive elements of wrong kinds of words. A worthwhile study is to go through Proverbs and mark those passages dealing with words, the mouth, the lips, and the tongue.

We must never speak words that we don't want to become a part of our lives. Don't say things like, "My wife and I are so unhappy," or "My husband is stupid."

One middle-aged wife said, "Somebody has to keep my husband humble. He gets too much attention from others, and he needs to be brought down a peg or two. I know just how to straighten him out." And that woman reaps the consequences of her words by sowing strife in her marriage.

Every husband needs a wife who will build him up, not tear him down. It's no sin to encourage each other with sincere compliments. Surely there are more good things in your partner than there are bad things!

A divorced woman said, "My husband's been gone for over three years now. How I wish he would come back. The loneliness is unbearable. There are a million things I forgot to tell him. If I had only let him know how good he really was, in so many ways. What a fool I was! I could never learn to compliment him; I was always on his back, pointing out all his mistakes. I see now how some husbands and wives treat each other so coldly, and I want to scream at them, 'Wake up, before it's too late! Quit your sarcasm, and encourage each other.'"

In his booklet *Your Marriage Can Make It!*, David Wilkerson outlined ten simple steps to help make your marriage successful. Step 6, printed below, is called "Learn how to say 'I'm sorry'—and mean it!"

Love, according to God's Word, is learning how to say "I'm sorry."

An irate husband boasted, "I walked out on my wife last night. She is always right, and I'm always wrong. But not this time; I'm not going to let her walk all over me again. I know I'm right on this matter. I'm always the one who has to give in first. Well, this time I'm staying away until she crawls on her hands and knees and admits she's dead wrong."

Along with learning to say "I'm sorry," husbands and wives must learn how to say "I forgive." Jesus warned that the forgiveness of our heavenly Father depends on our forgiving those who trespass against us. (See Mark 11:25–26.)

Has your husband or wife cheated on you? Have you been wounded by adultery? Did you accidentally discover a secret affair? Was there a true repentance? Are you trying hard to forgive and forget?

If he or she has shown evidence of godly sorrow—and every effort is being made to make it up to you—you must forgive. More than that, you must stop, once and for all, bringing up the past. Multiplied thousands of marriages have survived infidelity, but only because godly sorrow for sin was followed by Christlike forgiveness.[1]

The Bible instructs, *"The discretion of a man makes him slow to anger, and his glory is to overlook*

1. David Wilkerson, "Your Marriage Can Make It!" © 1979 World Challenge, Inc., PO Box 260, Lindale, Texas 75771.

a transgression" (Proverbs 19:11). And Jesus Himself taught us clearly,

> *Whenever you stand praying, if you have anything against anyone, forgive him, that your Father in heaven may also forgive you your trespasses. But if you do not forgive, neither will your Father in heaven forgive your trespasses.*
> (Mark 11:25–26)

God is very much interested in helping our marriages. He gave us the blueprint in His Word, and it's now up to us to trust His grace to enable us to achieve success. Satan is viciously opposed to our marriage success. He sows seeds of fear, wrong speaking, and defeatist attitudes to rob us of all that is good and designed for our happiness. Give no place to fear—even the fear of divorce and its subsequent miseries.

Love and Fear

There is a sentence in the book of Malachi that bothered me and started me studying this theme. *"A son honoureth his father, and a servant his master: if then I be a father, where is mine honour? and if I be a master, where is my fear?"* (Malachi 1:6 KJV). Notice the line, "Where is my fear?" Now turn to Malachi 3:16:

> *Then those who feared the LORD spoke to one another, and the LORD listened and heard them; so a book of remembrance was written before Him for those who fear the LORD and who meditate on His name.*

I noticed that all through the old covenant, the word *fear* is used in this sense. And then I saw the light. God commanded His people in Deuteronomy 6:5, *"You shall love the LORD your God with all your heart, with all your soul, and with all your strength."*

Natural man cannot do this. He can fear, but he cannot love. So why did God command him to love? That is God's method of teaching him what he really is. Until man receives eternal life, he cannot love—he can only fear.

Our evangelistic appeal has been largely based upon fear. We have mixed law and grace. We have tried to preach grace from the Old Testament—a very difficult thing to do. I heard a minister say years ago, "We have got to get the fear of God into the hearts of these people." He was wrong. He should have said, "We have got to get the love of God into the hearts of these sinners."

Fear has torments. Love brings joy. It is vitally important that we know the distinction between love and fear. The natural man fears God. The new creation man loves Him. (See Deuteronomy 10:12; Psalm 111:10; Ecclesiastes 12:13; Jeremiah 32:40; Exodus 14:31; Deuteronomy 28:58.)

Now you can understand that the covenant of works had a law for natural man and to govern the works of natural man. Natural man feared God. He obeyed as slaves obey. Fear ruled the people. "Obey the law or die" made good people out of bad ones. They feared to do evil unless they did it secretly.

The man who walks in love does right because he loves right. The new creation is ruled by love because the love nature of God is within. The new creation is born of God.

Fear Produces in Kind

O ne day, I made a house call to pray for a blind man. While I was there, he told me the following story.

"For many years of my life, I had perfect sight. Yet, even then, I had this fear within me that someday I would lose my sight. It haunted me often. Then came the time when my sight began to fade. My fears were enlarged. Doctors told me I would need glasses to aid my vision but nothing more serious. Yet this nagging, tormenting fear increased. I feared that I would not just stop at failing vision. I was grossly afraid I would completely lose my sight and that someday I would be in total darkness. Surely enough, the day came when I completely lost my sight, and I have been blind here in my home for several years."

When I heard this story, I was reminded of Job's experience, which contains an important warning for all of us. Job lost his health, his family, his possessions—everything. Like the blind man, Job was a victim of cruel fear. Look at how he explained his experience: "*The thing I greatly feared has come upon me, and what I dreaded has happened to me*" (Job 3:25).

Why is fear so powerful? How can fear produce those things we do not desire? We need to understand that fear is satanic. "*For God has not given us a spirit of fear, but of power and of love and of a sound mind*" (2 Timothy 1:7). When you begin to fear, you are giving place to the devil. Satanic fear develops more fear. And the spirits of fear can literally torment, snare, and captivate.

You must learn to deal with fear in its earliest stages, to resist it, to cast it out; refuse to give place to it. This can be done through the name of Jesus, by the empowering of the Holy Spirit, and upon the authority of God's Word.

Job testified that he had greatly feared the calamity that came upon him. Small fears, if not checked, develop into great fears. The greater the fears, the more readily they develop. The devil, who is a deceiver, works in subtle ways to brainwash people into accepting his evil works.

"*Lovers of Themselves*"

One of the signs of the last days is that "*men will be lovers of themselves*" (2 Timothy 3:2). This spirit is prevalent today; surely we are living in the last times. A manifestation of this spirit is the fear of sickness. If you are sick, get rid of any self-centeredness. Selfishness is not the climate for victorious faith to be operative. Faith works by love. (See Galatians 5:6.)

I regularly counsel people who have horrible fears of ill health. They are always looking for symptoms of some kind of disease. They almost seem to enjoy imaginary illness, and they speak of it with relish. These folks love to talk to you about their operations, their accidents, and their experiments with different diets, pills, fads, and remedies.

When you are filled with the fear of disease, you invariably concentrate upon disease, and that fear produces all kinds of sickness. I recently read a statement by a prominent medical authority that most nervous breakdowns are caused by imaginary illnesses.

Get rid of that image of illness, and begin to see yourself in the light of God's Word as a strong, healthy, vibrant person. Hold that image by confessing God's Word, which declares, *"By His stripes we are healed"* (Isaiah 53:5).

This fear of sickness produces self-coddling in your bid to get sympathy and pity. But, hear me, sympathy and pity will never help you; they will never minister healing and health to you. They will only produce the very thing you fear.

Not Bound by Hereditary Laws

Very often, I have counseled people who have become stricken with cancer and who have told me that they feared cancer into being. The devil brainwashed them into believing that because other members of their family had cancer, they would have it, too. This same spirit of fear manifests itself in heart attack victims and with other diseases.

While I acknowledge the power of the law of heredity, I acknowledge a greater law, which is the law of life in Christ Jesus. (See Romans 8:2.) New life in Jesus. Abundant life. It is vitally important that we do not give place to fear. When we do, the thing we greatly fear can come upon us.

Fear makes its play in unsound thoughts in the area of the mind. But God gives us a "*sound mind*" (2 Timothy 1:7) that learns to resist fear. Fear can cause a car wreck; with fear, you could be opening the way for Satan to involve you in an accident. Fear a cancer, and you could be paving the way to be afflicted with foul cancer. Fear a heart attack, and satanic spirits can unquestionably produce a genuine heart attack.

The famous American physician Dr. Alexis Carroll stated, "Fear is capable of starting a genuine disease." Many other medical authorities verify this fact. Job testified to it. The blind man I visited confirmed it. This is why you must get rid of your fears, lest your fears destroy you.

Fear failure, and you will likely fail. Fear the countenance of man, and you will ensnare your soul. Fear some sickness, and you will increase the prospect of a deadly malady vexing your life. Fear old age, and old age can be a terrible experience. Fear the loss of affection of your loved one, and you could be opening the way for opposing powers to assail.

Fear is no joke. It is a Bible fact. It is constantly verified by medical doctors and psychiatrists. Fear produces in kind. It has power—power to torment and snare your soul; power to paralyze your potential, to render you ineffective, and to handicap you in life; power to produce in kind.

Remember that this fear is not a mental quirk but an actual spirit that emanates from the adversary. *"For you did not receive the spirit of bondage again to fear"* (Romans 8:15). Look what Job's fears reaped for him: defeat, depression, destruction, disease, and disaster. The Bible commands us, *"Nor give place to the devil"* (Ephesians 4:27). When you give place to fear, you are giving place to the devil.

Resist fear in Jesus' name. Plead the blood of Jesus against every fear. Quote the words of God aloud against diabolical fear.

Being Independent of Circumstances

O ur Father God never intended that any of His children should be in bondage to circumstances or to people. Not only has He redeemed them out of the hand of Satan, but He has also given them His own nature and His own ability so that they become masters instead of slaves. They are meant to be the controlling element of every force in the world.

"For I have learned in whatever state I am, to be content: I know how to be abased, and I know how to abound" (Philippians 4:11–12). The Twentieth Century translation says, *"For I have learned in whatsoever state I am therein to be independent of circumstances."* I have learned to remember that in whatever state I am in, my Father is greater than all.

This is the song of victory: *"Now thanks be to God who always leads us in triumph in Christ"* (2 Corinthians 2:14). This was Paul's experience. No matter whether he was in jail or on a ship amid a storm that meant its utter destruction, he stood before the world a master, a conqueror. He was fearless because he was linked to omnipotence.

We ought to remember Proverbs 3:5–6: "*Trust in the LORD with all your heart, and lean not on your own understanding; in all your ways acknowledge Him* [or give Him His place], *and He shall direct your paths.*" How many times men are driven to extremity, where their own wisdom and ability are of no avail! Then, they cast all their anxieties and cares upon Him, for He cares for them. (See 1 Peter 5:7.) We come to our wits' end and we do not know what steps to take; then, He becomes our Light and our Deliverance.

Jesus told us in John 8:12, "*I am the light of the world. He who follows Me shall not walk in darkness, but have the light of life.*" This is a new kind of light. It is wisdom. It is ability. It is the thing that Jesus had in His earthly walk that made Him the most outstanding Man who ever lived.

There has never been a time when the heart of man has needed inward light as it needs it now. Our reasoning faculties, which find all their resources in the five senses, have limitations that give us a sense of failure, an inferiority complex. It is then that the inward light of the Spirit becomes our only guide. How we should cultivate that inward light! Learn to depend upon it, because it is so much safer than our reasoning faculties.

We should remember Psalm 23:1: "*The LORD is my shepherd; I shall not want.*" I like to put this verse in the present tense: "I do not want." He is my Shepherd, my Lord. He is the One who has guaranteed my protection, my care; in the presence of my enemies, I can feast in perfect security. You see, our God is bigger, greater, and wiser than any of our enemies, so we can fearlessly trust in Him.

The promise in Psalm 27:1 belongs to us: "*The LORD is the strength of my life; of whom shall I be afraid?*" Perhaps you know someone in the army who is facing death all the time. Here is the strength for your life. Here is the thing that will take fear from you and shield you from bullets, shrapnel, and every danger. You see, your enemies are dealing with God when they are dealing with you, because you and God are linked up together. Remember this. Remember that in every danger spot, He is the strength of your life; He is your ability.

My heart comes back to Paul's question in 2 Corinthians 2:16: "*Who is sufficient for these things?*" He answered, "*Our sufficiency is from God*" (2 Corinthians 3:5). This means that your ability, your wisdom, and the "something" that makes you superior to circumstances and environment are from Him. Yes, it makes you superior to physical weakness. You are in touch with God. You and God are tied up together.

Finally, let us consider Isaiah 41:10: *"Fear not, for I am with you."* It is the voice of my Father to everyone who is in harm's way. He wants you to know that He is your God. No matter what the opposition or what the danger may be, He is yours and you are His. He will guide you with His eyes upon you. (See Psalm 32:8.)

He will shield you from every danger. No one can touch you. Ten thousand may fall at your right hand, but it will not come near you. (See Psalm 91:7.) You are under His protection. Rest in Him with utter abandon. Trust Him with joyful confidence. He will never fail you.

To Him Who Overcomes

I n my travels as an evangelist, I have found that multitudes of people are oppressed by worry, insomnia, nervousness, sexual impurities, and many other disturbances. I have often stated that too many Christians are plagued by CDTs—cares, difficulties, and troubles. While the term *CDTs* may sound amusing, there is absolutely nothing amusing about the results they bring upon people's lives.

There are times when life is full of frustrations and we seem to be plagued with problems. Yet Jesus, who is our strength in the midst of these times, gave us a very blessed promise to help in our bold Bible living against these negative situations. He said, *"To him who overcomes I will grant to sit with Me on My throne, as I also overcame and sat down with My Father on His throne"* (Revelation 3:21). What a marvelous promise! Jesus has actually promised us a seat with Him on His throne for all time if we will be overcomers.

Free from Worry and Nervousness

Many people are bothered by worry and nervousness. Multitudes of people go through life needlessly worrying about everything. But worry can't help you. Worry never solved a problem, never paid a bill, and never healed a sickness. Remember to put the Lord first! Jesus said,

> *Which of you by worrying can add one cubit to his stature?...Therefore do not worry, saying, "What shall we eat?" or "What shall we drink?" or "What shall we wear?" For after all these things the Gentiles seek. For your heavenly Father knows that you need all these things. But seek first the kingdom of God and His righteousness, and all these things shall be added to you.* (Matthew 6:27, 31–33)

Then, look at Psalm 55:22: "*Cast your burden on the LORD, and He shall sustain you; He shall never permit the righteous to be moved.*" What have you to worry about if you cast all your problems on Him? God has the answers to those problems, and He can work them out easily. Put your trust in Jesus right now, and let all your worries roll onto Him.

The same thing applies when you suffer nervousness. Nervousness is just an outgrowth of worry and a lack of trust in God. What a great plague this is to many lives! How people are driven into fretting and stewing over problems, persons, or situations that may not be real causes for anxiety. Read Psalm 91.

> *He who dwells in the secret place of the Most High shall abide under the shadow of the Almighty. I will say of the LORD, "He is my refuge and my fortress; my God, in Him I will trust."…He shall cover you with His feathers, and under His wings you shall take refuge.*
> (Psalm 91:1–2, 4)

You won't be nervous and upset if you will learn how to dwell in God's secret place, under His wings. You ask, "How can I dwell there?" By reading His Word and by believing it! God is in His Word. When you put yourself into the shelter of His truth, He is there with you. I challenge you to look at His Word, to read it, to focus your attention on it, to believe it, and to dwell in it. When you do these things, victory over worry and nervousness will be yours, and much more besides!

Freedom from a Sense of Worthlessness

The devil is a specialist in his field of sowing seeds of self-pity into the minds of Christians. He focuses your attention upon disappointments you have experienced, or he emphasizes your lacks, weaknesses, failures, shortcomings, and mistakes. He brainwashes you to believe that you are the worst off of everybody.

A woman whose doctor diagnosed a tumor in her stomach became convinced that "my tumor is the biggest and most severe of anyone." A man I know feels sorry for himself because he is not as tall or as attractive as his neighbor. All of these feelings of self-pity are satanically induced, "*for we are not ignorant of his devices*" (2 Corinthians 2:11).

The devil tells you that you are not blessed as much as some other Christian, but that is a lie of the old deceiver. How much are you blessed? God has an answer for that. He says in Ephesians 1:3 that you are blessed "*with every spiritual blessing in the heavenly places in Christ.*" Absolutely, you are blessed as much as anyone else you know! You are blessed with every spiritual blessing. How can you beat that? Begin now to regard your life as one highly favored by God, richly blessed by Him. God says so, so it is.

Perhaps you protest, "I don't feel especially blessed." Feelings have nothing to do with this declaration of God's Word. Feelings or no feelings, God's Word says that you are blessed, so you are blessed! "*The just shall live by faith*" (Romans 1:17).

Anytime the devil grips you with feelings of self-pity, know that God has provided you with victory over the spirit of defeatism. "*Thanks be to God who always leads us in triumph in Christ*" (2 Corinthians 2:14). Pity yourself? No! Praise the Lord? Yes!

There is a divine ingredient in the power of praise that will expel the satanic device of self-pity and allow you to overcome it.

Freedom from a Bad Temper

I remember one time, years ago, when I saw a famous preacher lose his temper and damage his influence on an unsaved man who was interested in salvation. As Christians, we must always be on guard, lest by a loss of temper we would bring dishonor to the gospel. *"He who is slow to anger is better than the mighty, and he who rules his spirit than he who takes a city"* (Proverbs 16:32).

God calls it a virtue to be slow to anger. Some people pride themselves on their quick tempers. But God says that if this is your spirit, you are a fool! *"Do not hasten in your spirit to be angry, for anger rests in the bosom of fools"* (Ecclesiastes 7:9). This is God's Word: anger rests in the bosom of fools.

Now, if this is your case, perhaps it is because you are not truly born again—you have not been regenerated. You can obtain salvation today by repenting of your sins and by believing that the Lord Jesus Christ died on the cross for those sins, rising again so that you might live eternally. (See Romans 10:9.)

Or, you may be born again but not have been baptized in the Holy Spirit. This, too, can be taken care of as you read God's Word and accept His promise for yourself. (See Acts 2:38–39.)

If you are already a Christian, don't attempt to justify your wrong spirit. Some people try to explain away their tempers by saying, "Oh, that's my Irish blood," or "That's the German in me," or "That's the Indian in me going on the warpath." However, if we are new creatures in Christ, and we are walking in the Spirit, then old things have passed away, and all things about us will become new.

Psalm 37 has long been a favorite of mine. This psalm gives the command, *"Cease from anger, and forsake wrath; do not fret; it only causes harm"* (verse 8). God says, *"Cease from anger."* Put it away from your life. Let the Spirit of God cultivate the fruit of the Spirit in your heart to replace that anger. *"The fruit of the Spirit is love, joy, peace, longsuffering, kindness, goodness, faithfulness, gentleness, self-control. Against such there is no law"* (Galatians 5:22–23).

Boldly overcome your anger. *"He who overcomes shall inherit all things, and I will be his God and he shall be My son"* (Revelation 21:7).

The Conquest of Fear and Worry

I would like to conclude this chapter with a challenge from Forrest E. Smith, a pastor from Arkansas.

"We are living in the closing days of time. Even if we ministers never mentioned it, doubtless many would realize it because of the terrible oppression of the enemy, and through appalling acts of sin openly flaunted before our conscience-seared nation.

"The battle between spirit and flesh has reached such a screaming pitch that even once-stable Christians are floundering, being deceived or overpowered by the world. As nations pitted against each other work secretly to develop new weapons of horror, each struggling to produce the most devastating bomb or chemical, so the legions of darkness feverishly work against time, bringing spiritual weapons to bear against the children of God. Into this bitter struggle, the devil has injected his most demoralizing weapon of all: *fear.*

"Several years ago, I heard a friend say, 'I don't know what is wrong with me, but I have a feeling of dread in my soul. There is fear in my heart!' At that time, I thought that the Holy Spirit was sending conviction into his heart and that he needed to repent. I know now that my judgment was critical and unjust. My friend was being oppressed by a spirit of fear.

"Many people are being confused in these hours. We need to realize that there is a great difference between Holy Spirit conviction and evil spirit oppression. If the Holy Spirit convicts us, the heaviness of heart will depart when we have repented of the hasty word or thoughtless action that brought the conviction. God's Word plainly says, '*If we confess our sins, He is faithful and just to forgive us our sins and to cleanse us from all unrighteousness*' (1 John 1:9).

"However, after we are cleansed, the enemy may come along to dig up the matter again and oppress us with a spirit of fear for our very salvation; he may cause us to doubt our baptism in the Holy Spirit, or our healing. We may find ourselves pleading for forgiveness that was granted long ago. This is a spirit of fear and should be recognized and combated as such. It is the oppression of the devil.

"Such oppression drives men and women to destroy themselves in despair. It causes them to mistrust each other, to doubt God and His Word, and to question the reality of salvation and spiritual

211

things. This oppression is a sharp, terrifying, accusing voice that threatens to smother prayer under a blanket of unbelief. And it is not from God! *'For God has not given us a spirit of fear, but of power and of love and of a sound mind'* (2 Timothy 1:7). God has given us the spirit of power!

"Power over what? Jesus said to the disciples, *'Behold, I give unto you power...over all the power of the enemy'* (Luke 10:19 KJV). In Acts 1:8, we learn that we shall receive power to witness. In 1 John 4:4, we learn that we are of God and have already overcome the devil, *'because He who is in you is greater than he who is in the world.'* A person who is saved has already overcome the devil to the extent of being saved. If we can overcome the devil on one front, we can overcome him on all fronts.

"God told Joshua, *'No man shall be able to stand before you all the days of your life'* (Joshua 1:5). And we have that same God within our hearts! Only now, we have better promises and a more sure word of testimony than Joshua had. (See Hebrews 8:6.) If Joshua under the law could be strong and of good courage, how much more shall we who are under grace? God has not given us the spirit of fear, but the spirit of power—power to work, power to witness, and power to overcome the devil on every front.

"And God has given us the spirit of love. Love is not one of our natural attributes. It is an attribute of

God—'*God is love*' (1 John 4:8). Galatians 5:22 tells us that love is a fruit of the indwelling Spirit of Christ. Love is a powerful force, greater than anything the devil has concocted. Love is the way to conquer fear, for '*perfect love casts out fear*' (1 John 4:18). Not that we cease to reverence God, but that we cease to fear judgment on sins that have already been forgiven.

"Love covers a multitude of sins. It covered our sins with Jesus' blood and washed them away completely so that there is no longer any record of them in heaven. And that same love will help us to be patient with a lot of things our loved ones and fellow Christians do. We won't mind the off-key singing by some anointed but untalented saint. We won't be prideful, for love '*is not puffed up*' (1 Corinthians 13:4).

"And God has given us the spirit of a sound mind. With the spirit of a sound mind, we will recognize the tactics of the devil and will measure every vision and revelation by the Word of God. A sound mind will realize that the 'extra touch' required in the pulpit is simply more of God's Spirit and not some spectacular program hatched up to exalt man and draw greater crowds. Paul said in 2 Corinthians 2:11 that we are not ignorant of Satan's devices. We are aware that we fight against principalities and powers with which God alone can cope.

"Therefore, let us stay clear of unscriptural and unsound practices, and let us live by the revealed truth of God. When the enemy comes in like a flood, let God lift up a standard against him. (See Isaiah 59:19.) When he seeks to oppress with the spirit of fear, don't remain passive—rebuke him! Don't spend a lot of time arguing with him, for God has given us authority over the situation. God has given us the perfect antidote for fear. It is the spirit of power, of love, and of a sound mind."

Summary

Just remember the following, and move on to rise above fear and live in total victory!

1. Fear has one source—the devil. *"For God has not given us a spirit of fear, but of power and of love and of a sound mind"* (2 Timothy 1:7).

2. Notice that fear is not a mental quirk, but an actual spirit that emanates not from God but from the adversary: *"For you did not receive the spirit of bondage again to fear"* (Romans 8:15).

3. The results of fear are not pleasant. In fact, fear produces deep discomfort: *"Fear involves torment"* (1 John 4:18). Victims of satanic fear actually suffer physical agony, mental anguish, and spiritual torment.

4. Fear is deceptive; it leads people into snares of the enemy. *"The fear of man brings a snare"* (Proverbs 29:25). Fear beguiles, deludes, and leads people astray into a make-believe world of deception.

5. Fear produces in kind. You fear cancer, and that spirit of fear can actually produce cancer. Fear calamity, and you can be writing your own ticket for calamity. Fear failure, and you are opening the door for failure to envelop your life. Dare to rebuke fear in the name of Jesus. Call the spirit of fear by its right names: a deceiver, a liar, a faker, and a fraud. *"Resist the devil and he will flee from you"* (James 4:7).

6. Fear causes you to expect the bad. It can lead to an urge to commit suicide. Fear is manifested in stinginess toward God in your giving. Fear creates nervous breakdowns, sleeplessness, oppression in your prayer life, and bondage in witnessing.

7. No more convincing testimony is on record than that of Job, who said, *"The thing I greatly feared has come upon me, and what I dreaded has happened to me"* (Job 3:25). Defeat, depression, destruction, and even death were the results of his fears! Give no place to fear. Resist it in Jesus' name. Plead the blood. Quote the Word. Praise the Lord!

Finances and Stewardship

An Open Letter to Family Providers

I f you are a father and the provider for your family, I know how your honest spirit responds to the challenging words of 1 Timothy 5:8: *"If anyone does not provide for his own, and especially for those of his household, he has denied the faith and is worse than an unbeliever."*

For the first eleven years that I was the provider for the Don Gossett family, I experienced continual financial hardships and difficulties. Becoming the proud and happy father of five children by the time I was twenty-eight compounded my problems, of course, for there were unrelenting financial requirements. Inability to meet my commitments on time often produced embarrassment. Those unexpected expenditures labeled "emergency" drained my resources and kept my back up against the wall.

In 1961, we were living in the beautiful island city of Victoria, British Columbia. Our financial situation was so deplorable, however, that it was hardly a pleasant experience. Then, something happened

218

in the month of October that changed our picture of financial matters. Since that night, God has ministered to us and through us to meet *every* need for the last forty years!

It was an all-night prayer meeting that changed things for us. My wife and I poured out our hearts to God. I will never forget my wife's prayers that night. I had never heard anyone talk so frankly to our heavenly Father. It wasn't just a nagging, complaining series of utterances, either. As we concluded that night of prayer, we were confident that our needs would always be met from that night onward. And they have been, praise God!

God gave me a "secret" of faith for family finances that has never failed. The Lord revealed to me how I had limited Him in ministering to my needs because I constantly talked about my lack of money, my unpaid bills, and my other problems. God asked me a question from Amos 3:3: "*Can two walk together, unless they are agreed?*" I couldn't walk with God in financial supply if I disagreed with Him.

How was I disagreeing with God? By disagreeing with His Word. I changed my confession and said, "Never again will I confess lack, for '*my God shall supply all your need according to His riches in glory by Christ Jesus*' (Philippians 4:19)!" This Word of God became my new testimony. I agreed with God; I disagreed with the devil, who was keeping his oppressive hands on our finances. Never again have I been victimized by a lack of money for my family.

These are principles I have learned from God's Word. God honors hard, diligent work. Labor is often God's way of meeting needs. Many times, God has met my needs by my writings. Writing is hard work. Sitting up all night on a train to deliver a manuscript to a publisher is tedious. But even more rewarding than the financial returns are the hundreds of reports of lives transformed by this message.

You also need faith, not just work. Your faith is detectable by your words. "*Since we have the same spirit of faith, according to what is written, 'I believed and therefore I spoke,' we also believe and therefore speak*" (2 Corinthians 4:13). Faith is released and expressed by your mouth. Speak your faith. That is, speak the Word. Say often, "My God will supply all my needs." Those seven words will put you over, even as they have put me over financially. God absolutely watches over His Word to perform it.

There is no doubt about it: what you say is what you get. Speak of your lack of money, of how hard things are going for you, and you will get what you say. I urge you to confess often, "I have faith for finances for my family. Thank You, Father, for those riches." With your palms open, reach out to your Father and receive from Him.

Are You a Faithful Steward?

The Word tells us a lot about stewardship. When we think of stewardship, the phrase that normally comes before our minds is the stewardship of money. But after we are born from above, God says to us, "*You are not your own….You were bought at a price*" (1 Corinthians 6:19–20).

Paul told us that we are love-slaves of Jesus Christ. (See Romans 6:16–22.) Paul looked upon himself not as a servant, as we think of the word *servant*, but as a love-slave. That Greek word, *doulos*, means more than a purchased slave. It means a love-slave, some-one who serves because love compels him. Just as a mother becomes the love-slave of the home and the father becomes the love-slave of the family, so Paul became a love-slave of Jesus. He became a steward.

Now, a Christian must be a faithful steward. His time and his money are not his own. He holds them in trust. He uses them at the direction of the Master.

So many of us say, "I haven't time to go to the prayer meeting. I haven't time to study the Bible or take a correspondence course." You do not know the will of the Father, and you have been unable to find the will of the Master. Yet the will of the Father is shown in the Word. Had you known the Word, you would have known the will, and yet you say you haven't time.

That is the first thing in life. When we learn to put first things first, life becomes successful. The problem is that we have been putting secondary things, common things, in the first place. The most vital thing in the world is to know your Father, to know the Master, to know how to use the name of Jesus. You are a steward of the things you know.

Have you realized that you have the name of Jesus in your care and that the name has power even today to heal the sick, save the lost, and bring life and joy and gladness to human hearts? And yet you have never used it!

Perhaps you are like the one who hid the talent in the earth. (See Matthew 25:14–30.) You took care of it, you did not waste it, but you never used it. You are the custodian of an influence. Oh, the priceless value of influence!

Going by a tavern the other night, I saw a mother sitting at the bar drinking, and her little girl, not more than five, stood looking up wistfully at the mother. What an influence! The child's dream is to be like the mother.

We are stewards of our words—of our influence. What power is enwrapped in a single sentence. Homes are made by a sentence, and just a few words can destroy homes. They can give life and hope or death and anguish. We are stewards, and there is going to be a reckoning day. We will be asked what we have done with our responsibility.

Let us be faithful stewards, giving God His share of money, of time, of influence, and of our priceless words. Let us be faithful stewards of the power invested in the name of Jesus.

How Can I Get Ahead Financially?

Some people cannot get ahead financially and wonder if it is God's will for them to be poor, in order that they remain humble. But poverty is not God's will for your life. His Word says, "*I pray that you may prosper in all things and be in health, just as your soul prospers*" (3 John 2). God is not a poverty-stricken God, and He doesn't produce poverty-stricken children.

The Bible clearly reveals that it is Satan who is the devourer, the thief, and the destroyer. (See John 10:10.) He seeks to consume our resources, deplete our money, and exhaust our financial ability. You can, however, "*resist the devil and he will flee from you*" (James 4:7).

The good news announced by Jesus in Luke 4:18–19 included liberation from poverty. Therefore, you need not confess lack; instead, declare, "*My God shall supply all* [my] *need according to His riches in glory by Christ Jesus*" (Philippians 4:19). The words *insufficiency* and *inadequacy* need not be a part of your vocabulary.

Jesus came to give us life—and life "*more abundantly*" (John 10:10). This abundant life of Christ overflows into physical and material abundance, as well as spiritual abundance.

In Need of Employment

Many people in today's world are in need of good jobs. The Bible is filled with promises of provision, but there are certain conditions that you must meet.

1. "*Seek first the kingdom of God and His righteousness, and all these things shall be added to you*" (Matthew 6:33). As you put the Lord first in your life, Jesus promises to provide for your every need. It is important, however, that you establish proper priorities—that God and His work are number one in your life. "*As long as he sought the LORD, God made him prosper*" (2 Chronicles 26:5).

2. "*Delight yourself also in the LORD, and He shall give you the desires of your heart*" (Psalm 37:4). In this case, the desire of your heart is to find a job. So, delight yourself in the Lord by pleasing Him and praising Him.

3. "*This Book of the Law shall not depart from your mouth, but you shall meditate in it day and night, that you may observe to do according to all that is written in it. For then you will make your*

way prosperous, and then you will have good success" (Joshua 1:8). God has promised success and prosperity to the man or woman in whose heart the Word of God constantly abides.

As you continue to look for employment, remember that being wholehearted is essential to success in any endeavor. Anything less inevitably results in failure.

God loves you and has obligated Himself to supply your needs. (See Philippians 4:19.) Stand upon this promise. Confess this truth. Then leave the rest to God.

What if you already have a job but are looking for a better one? If this is the case, your heavenly Father knows that you need a better job in order to provide more adequately for your family, to give more generously to help spread the gospel, or to improve working conditions that are not suitable in your present employment.

Here are three steps to take that will bring God's response of a better job for you.

1. Be assured that "*your heavenly Father knows that you need all these things*" (Matthew 6:32).

2. With total assurance, cast your need for a better job upon the Lord who cares for you. "*Casting all your care upon Him, for He cares for you*" (1 Peter 5:7).

3. "*No good thing will He withhold from those who walk uprightly*" (Psalm 84:11). Because you walk uprightly before God, He will not withhold this "*good thing*"—your new and better job.

Finally, remember that "*as long as he sought the LORD, God made him prosper*" (2 Chronicles 26:5). Here is a key to prosperity from God: take time to seek the Lord in prayer, to study His Word, and to honor Him with your giving.

Do Not Worry about Financial Problems

Many Christians are robbed of their peace and joy in the Lord because of constant worries about money. However, if you are faithful in giving your tithes and offerings, you can claim God's promises to supply all your needs and free you from financial worries. Banks may close, money may be devalued, but God's Word is sure forever.

Read these ten reasons why you need never worry about money matters again:

1. "*For He Himself has said, 'I will never leave you nor forsake you'*" (Hebrews 13:5).

2. "*I have been young, and now am old; yet I have not seen the righteous forsaken, nor his descendants begging bread*" (Psalm 37:25).

3. "*Trust in the LORD, and do good; so shalt thou dwell in the land, and verily thou shalt be fed*" (Psalm 37:3 KJV).

4. *"If then God so clothes the grass, which today is in the field and tomorrow is thrown into the oven, how much more will He clothe you, O you of little faith?"* (Luke 12:28).

5. *"Seek the kingdom of God, and all these things shall be added to you"* (Luke 12:31).

6. *"Do not fear, little flock, for it is your Father's good pleasure to give you the kingdom"* (Luke 12:32).

7. *"No good thing will He withhold from those who walk uprightly"* (Psalm 84:11).

8. *"If you then, being evil, know how to give good gifts to your children, how much more will your Father who is in heaven give good things to those who ask Him!"* (Matthew 7:11).

9. *"Honor the LORD with your possessions, and with the firstfruits of all your increase; so your barns will be filled with plenty"* (Proverbs 3:9–10).

10. *"He who sows sparingly will also reap sparingly, and he who sows bountifully will also reap bountifully"* (2 Corinthians 9:6).

Another Scripture that should be included on this list is Malachi 3:10–11, but we will examine that passage in the section below through the case of a man named Alexander H. Kerr. He tested God's promise and received truly amazing results.

The Rising Cost of Fear

Many people today are being harassed in their financial situations. They fear the possibilities of spiraling inflation, a major recession, or both.

Often, Satan takes advantage of the financial anxieties of life and brings his choice spirit of fear to torment, to snare, and to incite all kinds of difficulties. Indeed, the matter of finances is like any other situation: what you fear is what you get! If you give place to the fear of financial failure, you invite that failure to come and grip your life. One sure way to conquer the fear of financial defeat is found in God's Word on giving from Malachi 3:8–11:

> *"Will a man rob God? Yet you have robbed Me! But you say, 'In what way have we robbed You?' In tithes and offerings. You are cursed with a curse, for you have robbed Me, even this whole nation. Bring all the tithes into the storehouse, that there may be food in My house, and try Me now in this," says the LORD of hosts, "if I will not open for you the windows of heaven*

229

and pour out for you such blessing that there will not be room enough to receive it. And I will rebuke the devourer for your sakes, so that he will not destroy the fruit of your ground, nor shall the vine fail to bear fruit for you in the field," says the LORD of hosts.

By standing on the Word of God and obeying it in giving our tithes and offerings, we can defeat the devourer's attacks on our finances. We can meet and defeat Satan by saying, "My God has promised to open the gates of heaven and pour out a greater blessing than I can receive. Satan, be gone, in Jesus' name!"

This is how one man learned that even fearful circumstances cannot break God's promise made to those who tithe. Alexander H. Kerr was converted under the ministry of Dwight L. Moody at the age of fourteen and joined the Presbyterian church in Philadelphia. In 1902, Mr. Kerr read a book called *Judah's Scepter and Joseph's Birthright* by Bishop Allen.

In his book, Bishop Allen referred to the vow Jacob made in Genesis 28:22: *"Of all that You give me I will surely give a tenth to You."* Twenty years later, this same Jacob returned to his home with servants and cattle in great abundance. Thus, he became one of the richest men of the East as a result of keeping his covenant of tithing to the Lord God.

With some doubts, but with a sincere desire to see if the Bible was true, and to prove beyond a doubt that there is a personal God whose promises are intended for the people of this day, Mr. Kerr made a special covenant on June 1, 1902, to set aside the tithe, or 10 percent of his income, for the work of the Lord.

At that time, he had a mortgage on his little home, owed many obligations, and was burdened with cares and worries, especially of a financial nature. However, he was determined to prove God as Jacob did and see that God "*is the same yesterday, today, and forever*" (Hebrews 13:8). He was challenged particularly by Malachi 3:7–18, but also by Proverbs 3:9–10, Leviticus 27:30–32, and Genesis 14:18–20.

Within three months after Mr. Kerr began to tithe, unexpected and unforeseen blessings came to him in great amounts! God opened his eyes to see His love and faithfulness to His promises, especially in regard to tithing.

According to Your Faith Let It Be to You

That same year, with very little capital, Mr. Kerr organized the firm known as the Kerr Glass Manufacturing Company. He had a strong faith in God's tithing promises contained in Malachi 3:10–12, and the Kerr Glass Manufacturing Company ultimately became one of the largest firms selling fruit jars in the United States.

The jars were manufactured in San Francisco. At the time of the San Francisco earthquake in

1906, this firm was manufacturing his fruit jars. Mr. Kerr had put practically every cent he had into this fruit jar enterprise, and then he received news of the earthquake. His friends came to him and said, "Kerr, you are a ruined man."

He replied, "I don't believe it; or if I am, then the Bible is not true. I know God will not go back on His promises." He wired to San Francisco and received the following reply: "Your factory is in the heart of the fire and undoubtedly is destroyed. The heat is so intense we will be unable to find out anything for some days."

What a time of testing this was! Mr. Kerr's faith in the Lord never wavered. He stood unmoved on the promise of Malachi 3:11: "*I will rebuke the devourer for your sakes, so that he will not destroy the fruit of your ground.*" About a week after the earthquake and fire, a second telegram arrived, saying, "Everything for a mile and a half on all sides of the factory burned; but your factory was miraculously saved."

God's Word Will Not Return to Him Void

Mr. Kerr immediately boarded a train for San Francisco. The factory was a two-story wooden building that contained the huge tanks where the glass was melted. The tanks were kept at a fierce 2,500 degrees, and oil was used for fuel. Therefore, this building was probably the most flammable in San Francisco.

232

The fire had raged on all sides of this glass factory, creeping up to the wooden fence surrounding the building and even scorching it. Then, the fire leaped around and over and beyond the building, burning everything in its path. However, not even the wooden fence was burned, and not a single glass jar was cracked by the earthquake or fire!

This was nothing short of a miracle of God's divine power in protecting a man who held his faith that God's promises made to those who tithe would never be broken by any circumstances.

In 1912, Mr. Kerr wrote his first leaflet on the subject of tithing, entitled "God's Cure for Poverty." This was followed by another tract, entitled "God's Loving Money Rule for Your Financial Prosperity." Every case of fruit jars that left the factory contained one of these leaflets. He also gave them away to people who would distribute them judiciously, bearing the entire cost himself. From 1912 until the time of his death in 1924, Mr. Kerr freely distributed more than five million of these leaflets!

Three weeks before his death, Mr. Kerr addressed the members of the First Baptist Church of Riverside, California, on the blessings and riches of tithing possessions, income, and increase. Every business in which he had an investment tithed. His returns were so great that he created a tithing fund and had it incorporated. His tithing gifts went around the world, for he was deeply interested in the distribution of Bibles and gospel literature.

Mr. Kerr rose from poverty to having millions because he believed that God would honor His promise to pour out His blessings today upon those who would accurately and carefully tithe, or set aside one-tenth of their possessions, salary, or income, for the Lord's work.

Do you have financial fears? Are you afraid to give? I challenge you: let the Lord give you a release from the fear of financial failure, which can often stare you in the face and cause you loss of sleep. Let's pray about it.

> Father, in the name of Jesus, I ask for the release from financial distress for myself and every friend united with me right now. Father, You know how real these fears are—the fear of financial disaster, the fear of inability to pay bills, and the fear of bankruptcy. I ask You to bring deliverance to every captive life, and I pray that the spirit of fear will be expelled. For You have said, *"Fear not, for I am with you"* (Isaiah 41:10). Thank You, Lord, for Your release, in Jesus' mighty name. Amen.

Now, receive your release and move on to prosperity!

Tithing

God is the original Giver. He so loved that He gave. (See John 3:16.) All giving is a love affair. When people love the Master, they will give to His cause. When they love the church, they will support it. When they love the message, they will bear the burden of its broadcasting.

Anyone who is not a giver does not have close fellowship with the Father. The relationship of giving to prayer is shown in 1 John 3:22. By closing up your heart to the needy, you close heaven to your prayers. The reason for many unanswered prayers is explained in this Scripture.

When we call for the doctor, we expect to pay him; when we get medicine at the drugstore, we expect to pay. We should share with the Lord when He answers our prayers, just as we share with the doctor or druggist. His blessing will always match our giving. I have found that the measure of my giving is the measure of my receiving. If we give largely, we will receive largely.

> *"Bring all the tithes into the storehouse, that there may be food in My house, and try Me now in this," says the LORD of hosts, "if I will not open for you the windows of heaven and pour out for you such blessing that there will not be room enough to receive it."*
> (Malachi 3:10)

This is a warning to the careless giver. It is a challenge to the earnest giver, and it is a promise to the real giver. God tells us to bring the whole tithe into the storehouse. Sometimes, it is very hard to give the whole tithe.

I remember a man telling me that he was always a tither and had been recently blessed because of it while he worked on a salary. He had saved up enough money to go into business, and his business was prosperous from the beginning. Instead of being able to give forty or fifty dollars a month, he was now able to give several hundred, and the temptation was strong to cut his giving down.

He was an honest man, and he prayed about it. Finally, he caught the vision and promised God that he would give a full tenth. Then, he began to give offerings beside the tenth. When I last saw him, instead of one small store, he had three large stores. The hand of God was upon him in a very rich way.

I knew of another who received several thousand dollars from his mother's estate. He had tithed in his small way until this large amount came in. He discussed it with his wife, prayed about it, and finally dared to give God His share. Then, God became their Partner in a sense they had never known.

God tells us that He wants us to bring the whole tithe into the storehouse so that there may be food for the poor and the needy. He says, "I want you to prove Me and see if I will not pour you out a blessing so large that you can hardly receive it." The next verse says,

> *"And I will rebuke the devourer for your sakes, so that he will not destroy the fruit of your ground, nor shall the vine fail to bear fruit for you in the field," says the LORD of hosts.*
> (Malachi 3:11)

Most of God's people put money in bags with holes. They often lose their investments because they will not share with the Lord. Yet if the Lord is a sharer in your income, it is in His interest to back you up and to protect you from losses.

Do not use your tithe for any other purpose; give it to the Lord. You cannot pay bills with it. You cannot support your own children with it. It is to be given to the Lord and to His work.

Generosity in Giving

The most joyful Christians are those who know the blessing of bold giving. I dare you to put God to the test in your giving. When you give in this manner, God has given you permission to affirm boldly, "I am proving my God. He is pouring out an overflowing blessing for me. He is rebuking the devourer for my sake!"

Harty Wiltbanks was one of the most successful Christians I have ever known. His testimony for Christ was strong and influential. During one crusade, my wife and I stayed in his home, and he told us his "success" story.

Shortly after coming out of World War I, unsaved and penniless, Wiltbanks received Christ as his Lord and Savior. Reading the Bible, he began to take God's Word at face value. He asked the Lord for a job and got one. He read God's promises concerning giving and began to tithe and give offerings, too. He was unwavering in his faith because he realized that "*God is not a man, that He should lie*" (Numbers 23:19), and therefore, God had to bless him, both spiritually and financially.

Wiltbanks began to receive abounding blessings. This continued through many years, and by giving, he was also instrumental in winning multitudes of souls. Now, he is home with the Lord, reaping his reward.

The Bible says that when we give, we are honoring the Lord. The result is God's promise that He will reward us with plenty. (See Proverbs 3:9–10.) When you give of your substance, recognize that you are actually honoring the Lord, and that you can expect the reward of plenty as God blesses you materially.

What is *bold* giving? It is generous giving (see Proverbs 11:25), bountiful giving (see 2 Corinthians 9:6), cheerful, ungrudging giving (see 2 Corinthians 9:7), blessed giving (see Acts 20:35), and devil-defeating giving (see Malachi 3:11).

What is the *blessing* of bold giving? It not only opens the windows of heaven (see Malachi 3:10), but its reward is "*given to you: good measure, pressed down, shaken together, and running over will be put into your bosom*" (Luke 6:38). God promises you that plenty will be your reward—spiritually and materially. But most important, your bold giving will send forth the gospel for the winning of souls and the meeting of needs.

The opposite of bold giving is *fearful* giving. "I was afraid to trust God's Word for many years," a

Christian man told me. "Fear compelled me to give dimes when I should have given dollars. I found no joy in giving because of this spirit. Finally, I began to give cheerfully, liberally, and ungrudgingly. How abundantly God began to bless me! I indeed found the blessing of *bold* giving, and how my Christian life has been transformed!"

Tithing with Abandonment

Dare to abandon yourself to God's promises in your giving. You will not only "*lay up for yourselves treasures in heaven*" (Matthew 6:20), but you will also experience tremendous joy here below. I have known many blessed people who have had the courage to give liberally in this manner and have seen God do wondrous deeds in response to their obedience to His Word. One such man was my friend, evangelist Velmer Gardner of California. His testimony of tithing has always blessed my heart.

"We were in the heart of the Great Depression. My father died and left no insurance, so it fell on my older brother and me to provide for our mother and five brothers and sisters. Men were out of work by the thousands. We were so poor that every morning, as I started to look for work, I would have to put cardboard inside my shoes to keep my feet off the ground. I couldn't afford five cents for shoestrings, so I used wire to keep my shoes on.

"One day, a friend came and said, 'I think I can get you a job in a big box factory.' I was thrilled.

240

Hundreds of men were trying to get jobs there every day, but he got me in. We were twenty-five miles from home at this factory and stayed in a little cabin by the river. I started to work for the tremendous sum of twenty dollars a week, which was really a lot of money in those days. God spoke to me all week about tithing.

"When I came home that Saturday night, I said, 'Mother, I feel that I should tithe. I know we're poor and need all I can earn, but I want to go on with God.' My mother cried and said, 'Son, you walk with God; He will take care of us.'

"On Sunday morning, I gave two dollars for my tithe, and that night, I put an offering of one dollar in the basket. Oh, how happy I was that I had obeyed God! Immediately, He began to bless my soul; the air seemed fresher, the grass greener, the flowers prettier; the birds sang more sweetly, and I felt better. Why? Because He was opening the windows of heaven upon my soul.

"I went happily to work the next day, and, when I arrived at the plant, there stood the foreman, waiting to see me. They called him 'Old Grump.' No one had ever seen him smile. He was the terror of the whole crew. He hollered, 'Come here, you.' The devil gave me the thought, 'Now, don't you wish you had those three dollars to get back to town? You're fired!'

"With fear and trembling, I stood before Old Grump. With a very stern look on his face, he said,

'I've been watching you work.' I was really scared. He continued, 'We just bought a new electric box-making machine—the first ever invented. My boy will operate it, and you will be his assistant. You'll receive a pay increase of 33 percent.'

"I shouted 'Hallelujah!' so loudly in my soul that the devil must have fallen over himself getting away from me! Saturday night, when I returned home, I joyfully announced, 'Mother, God has proven Himself. I got a raise!' That Sunday, I had more tithes to pay and a bigger offering to give.

"The next Monday morning, I went back to work, and, to my horror, there the boss stood again. The devil again gave me the thought, 'Now listen, you can just shove me away so far. You had to testify about what God did when you started tithing, but now you've lost your job. This is the end.'

"Again, with fear and trembling, I stood before Old Grump. He almost smiled as he said, 'We just bought another machine yesterday; you can operate this one. You will get twice as much money as you have been receiving.' The devil left on roller skates for hell! Within six weeks, I was making more money than any man who had been there for twenty years—including the boss himself.

"Don't tell me it doesn't pay to tithe! God will bless you financially, spiritually, and physically. Since that time, God has blessed me with health. He has taken care of my every need, the windows of heaven are still open, and His blessing is thrilling my soul. I would not stop tithing for anything in the world."

Luke 6:38 says, "*Give, and it will be given to you: good measure, pressed down, shaken together, and running over.*" God will give you what you deserve, then He will press it down, shake it together, and run it over. No wonder David said, "*My cup runs over*" (Psalm 23:5). Yours will, too, if you give to God.

When I was just a small, freckle-faced boy, I would walk up to the candy counter of the little grocery store and say, "Gimme a penny's worth of jelly beans!" The old grocery man's heart would move with compassion, and he would fill up a small bag with red and black jelly beans. As I saw the bag fill up, I wanted to get behind that counter, take the bag, and gently shake it. I knew that if I could, I'd be able to get a few more jelly beans to fit inside! I wanted all I could get.

Friends, that is exactly what God will do. He will press it down, shake it together, and run it over. Many Christians today believe in their hearts that tithing is right, but they listen to the devil's protests that with the rising cost of living, they cannot possibly afford to tithe and still provide for their families. Believe me, that is a lie from the father of lies himself. In a time when Satan's inflation is running rampant in the world, we only have God on our side to rebuke the devourer as we tithe in obedience to

His Word. There is no stronger foundation and no greater surety in this time of financial difficulties than the Word of God.

God Will Make Good His Promise

Even so, it often takes quite a bit for the impact of God's Word to reach some individuals. Here is the testimony of one dear country preacher named Brother Kuykendal, who learned the faithfulness of God's Word in an unusual way. He explained to his congregation how God dealt with him concerning the importance of tithing.

"Many years ago, when I was a country missionary, the famous Baptist businessman H. Z. Duke, who founded the Duke and Ayers nickel stores, came to this county to speak with Christian laymen. He urged men and women everywhere to try God and see if He would not make good on His promises to bless them in material things when they gave tithes and offerings to His cause. After Mr. Duke had spoken at one community, I took him in my buggy to another community.

"Mr. Duke said to me, 'Brother Kuykendal, do you believe in tithing?'

"'I certainly do,' I said. 'I believe in tithing, and I preach it myself.'

"'But Brother Kuykendal,' he continued, 'do you practice tithing?'

"Sadly, I had to answer, 'No, I do not. I believe in tithing, but I cannot practice it. You see, I have thirteen children at home. Every meal, fifteen of us sit down at the table. I receive only $125 per month, and I have to maintain my own horse and buggy for constant traveling. It is impossible to take care of all the needs of a family of fifteen with $125 a month and have money left to tithe. So I believe in tithing, and I preach it, but I cannot practice it.'

"Mr. Duke was a very kindly man. He said, 'Brother Kuykendal, would you like to tithe? Would you tithe if I backed you up financially so you could be sure you would not lose by it?'

"'Nothing would please me more,' I said.

"So, Mr. Duke made me the following proposition. 'For the next year, I want you to set out to give God at least $12.50 every month, as soon as you get your salary. Then, if you feel led, you may give more. I promise you that if you need help, I will give it. Simply write me a letter and say, "Brother Duke, I'm giving a tithe, but I miss the money. I need it for my family. I've given so much thus far." I promise you that I will send you a check by return mail. Are you willing to try tithing on that basis?'

"I hesitated a moment, moved with emotion, and Brother Duke said, 'I have thirty-two stores and plenty of money to make good on my promise. I will be glad to do it. Will you risk me and start tithing on the simple promise that I will make good any amount you've given, any time that you find you miss it and need it? Will you trust me about it?'

"I gladly accepted his offer. I said, 'Yes, Brother Duke, I've wanted to tithe for a long time, but I felt I simply could not do it. Now, thank God, I can tithe, and I'll be glad to. And I will not feel like a hypocrite when I tell others they ought to tithe.'

"So, I started tithing for the first time in my life. At the beginning of every month, I took out one-tenth of my salary and gave it to the Lord's cause; then, as I felt led, I gave more. In the back of my mind, I always had the thought, *Mr. Duke promised me that he would make it up any time I need it. He will send me the money if I simply ask him for it.*

"But a strange thing happened. It seemed our money went further than before. I would preach in some county community and somebody would tie a crate of chickens onto the back of my buggy. Somebody would put a ham under the seat. Or a godly woman would put some home-canned fruit in my buggy.

"A neighboring farmer said, 'Brother Kuykendal, God has blessed me so much that I cannot get all my corn in the crib this year. I have an extra wagonload that I cannot keep. May I put it in your crib for your buggy horse?' Another neighbor drove over with a large wagon full of hay for the cow.

"It was very strange, but that year we had no doctor bills. The children's clothes didn't seem to wear out so quickly. It was a happy time, and I never had to call on Mr. Duke to make up the money I had given to the Lord in tithes.

"One day, when the year was almost over, I suddenly realized with shame that I had believed what H. Z. Duke had said. He had promised to make good anything I lacked by tithing, and I had believed him. But my heavenly Father had made the same promise, and I had not believed Him. I had taken the word of a man when I did not take the promise of God!

"Now, I had proven God's promises and found that He had taken care of me and my big family on a small salary. I had found that $112.50 per month took care of our family better, with God's blessing, than $125 did without being under the blessed covenant that He has made with those who seek first the kingdom of God through tithes."

This godly country preacher stood there before the congregation, weeping. With deepest emotion, he said, "I have tithed for many, many years. My salary has increased year after year. We've always had enough, and we've never been shamed. The greatest spiritual blessing in my life, aside from salvation, has been in learning to trust God about daily needs for my home and our big family."

God has proven to everyone who has ever tried Him that He will keep His promise. He provides for those who bring Him the firstfruits, those who give tithes and offerings, and those who boldly seek first the kingdom of God and His righteousness, allowing the Lord to add blessings of abundance to their lives!

Giving Is the Basis of Receiving

I often wondered why some prayers were not answered. Then, I discovered the relationship of giving to receiving. Only givers are receivers. Only as you give do you have the capacity to receive. This is the law of love in action.

You may receive blessings and have your prayers answered at the beginning, but if you do not become a giver, your prayers will cease to be answered.

Giving and receiving are so closely allied throughout the Old and New Testaments that it behooves every child of God to keep a careful watch on his giving—the giving of money, the giving of tithes, the giving of love, the giving of time, and the giving of the Word.

I could give you many illustrations of people who prayed for healing and failed to get it until they began tithing. There would be more giving if we understood the blessings that come through it. Money is the smallest part of real giving—the giving of a friendly word or taking time to shake hands and smile.

Give your prayers! Oh, what it would mean if we gave life—if we gave of our prayer time. We would tell people about it. We would say gently, "I am praying for you. I was waiting before the Lord for you this morning."

How it would thrill the heart! We do not bear people's burdens as we ought to. We do not carry loads as we should. It is easy to give a dollar, but to give our time, love, and wisdom is to be blessed.

Jesus said, *"Freely you have received, freely give"* (Matthew 10:8). To us, He says, "I have given Myself to you with utter abandon. Now, I want you to give yourselves with utter abandon to others. I want you to give your whole being to the church and to the world."

What a challenge this is! Read carefully chapters eight and nine of 2 Corinthians. *"He who sows sparingly will also reap sparingly, and he who sows bountifully will also reap bountifully"* (2 Corinthians 9:6). Do you want a large harvest? Then give! Will not a large acreage yield a large harvest? You will give of your best if you want to get His best.

Jesus sent the disciples out and told them to heal the sick, to raise the dead, and to cast out demons. (See Matthew 10:5–8.) Christian worker, freely give your time to open the Scriptures until you know how to take what the Father has for you!

Financial Security

I n conclusion, remember that financial security and success is certain when you stand on God's promise to supply all your needs. (See Philippians 4:19.) Let your confession be:

- No matter how many unpaid bills I have, my God will supply all my need.

- Regardless of the condition of the economy, my God will supply all my need.

- Regardless of the size of my bank account, my God will supply all my need.

- When financial embarrassment stares me in the face, my God will supply all my need.

- Regardless of the tight money situation, my God will supply all my need.

- In spite of past financial failures, my God will supply all my need.

- When things appear all wrong, my God will supply all my need.

- When things appear all right, my God will supply all my need.
- Wherever I am, my God will supply all my need.

Praise, Love, and Prayer

Praise, the Password to Blessing

*Praising God and having favor with all the
people.*   (Acts 2:47)

The life of praising God is crowned with continual responses from heaven. One of the
delightful benefits of praising God is *"having favor with all the people."* For years now, I have
daily endeavored to obey the hundreds of commands to praise the Lord. The Lord has manifested
His awesome power, giving me favor with people.

Interstate 5 stretches from the Mexican border,
all through California, Oregon, and Washington, to
the border of Canada. The last miles are in Blaine,
Washington. An elderly couple owned the land for
those final miles to Canada. When the construction
of this superhighway was completed, the Blaine couple still owned two valuable pieces of property on
both sides of I-5.

A businessman called me and said, "Mr. Gossett,
the couple who owns the land where I-5 was built

have two tracts of land on either side. They want to give it to you. However, they want it to be an anonymous gift, and you will never know your benefactors. Would you accept this gift of great value?"

I was overwhelmed with delight! I never learned the names of the gracious couple, as they requested. But it was the law of cause and effect in operation. The life of daily praise was the cause; the favor with the people was God's doing.

Words of heartfelt praise to our Lord are the passwords to blessing. Favor is one of His choice blessings! We don't praise God to manipulate Him to grant favor. Praise is obedience. Favor is His loving gift to us for healing, finances, family blessings, and all the abundance that only God can give.

How Love Acts

Love *"does not seek its own"* (1 Corinthians 13:5). That is the law of love. Selfishness is always seeking its own. Love lives for others. *"He died for all, that those who live should live no longer for themselves, but for Him who died for them and rose again"* (2 Corinthians 5:15).

Love is always strong and never weak. Romans 15:1–3 tells us that love bears the infirmities of others. Galatians 6:2 says, *"Bear one another's burdens, and so fulfill the law of Christ."* That is the law of love. When you see someone carrying a load that is too heavy for him, you get under it with him. You help him bear the load. We have in our assembly men and women who live just like this. They bear one another's burdens. They help pay each other's rent.

> *As the Father loved Me, I also have loved you; abide in My love. If you keep My commandments, you will abide in My love, just as I have kept My Father's commandments and abide in His love.* (John 15:9–10)

Jesus lived in His Father's love. He kept His Father's word. His commandment to us is that we love one another. (See John 13:34.) When we walk in that love and keep that commandment, what a blessing we immediately become to others! First Peter 2:21–24 gives us a picture of walking in the steps of the Master. Read this Scripture over and over again until it becomes a part of your life.

> *To this you were called, because Christ also suffered for us, leaving us an example, that you should follow His steps: 'Who committed no sin, nor was deceit found in His mouth'; who, when He was reviled, did not revile in return; when He suffered, He did not threaten, but committed Himself to Him who judges righteously; who Himself bore our sins in His own body on the tree, that we, having died to sins, might live for righteousness—by whose stripes you were healed.* (1 Peter 2:21–24)

Now, turn to Ephesians 5:1–2: *"Be imitators of God as dear children. And walk in love."* Every step outside of love is a failure. The man who constantly walks in love will never sin. Sin is stepping out of love. An essential command for believers is to love one another even as Christ has loved you.

And as you walk in love, you walk in the light. You walk in God, and that walk will never let you be selfish or unkind or bitter; it will lead you to be just like the Master.

"Study to Be Quiet"

How hard it is to sit down and be quiet—to keep the hands and feet still and the heart from tumultuous rebellion! We are nervous and restless, overworked by worry. When we study, our minds leap from place to place, from subject to subject. We lie down at night to rest, and the mind keeps on thumping and throbbing like a tireless engine.

The apostle Paul said, "*Study to be quiet*" (1 Thessalonians 4:11 KJV), or, as the literal Greek reads, "Be ambitious to be quiet." This is a new ambition! Why does he say this? Because in your quietness will be your strength and assurance. (See Isaiah 30:15.)

Great strength is found only in quietness. The quiet man makes the strong leader; the quiet mother makes the strong anchor of the home. Can one be quiet today with all the pressure of business, society, poverty, and the struggle for dollars? Yes.

There is a private inner sanctuary in every soul. And into this private inner sanctuary we can go for a little while, even amid the distractions and galling worries that press in upon us. Now, I think of three things that will help us in this.

First, we must *study* to be quiet. We must put our minds to it. We must keep saying to ourselves, "Be quiet, now." Be calm, speak softly, watch your voice, and keep that sharp tone out of it.

Second, we must draw our quietness and strength from God. Say to your soul, "I breathe in God's holy calmness. I drink deeply at the eternal springs of soul silence. I renew my physical and mental strength at the fountain of restfulness. I look at the calm face of Jesus as He climbs Golgotha, as they nail Him to the cross, and I cry out, 'Your calmness, O Christ, is mine.'"

Third, we must put out of our houses, hearts, and lives the noisy children of jealousy and the bitter visitor of strife. Order selfishness to leave your home at once, never to sit at your table again. Cut down every quarrelsome tree; have no place for sulking. Say good-bye to supersensitiveness and your own self-gratification, and rise up into the holy atmosphere of living for someone else. Remember that he who does not live for himself accumulates joy, rest, and quietness.

So, as you start out today, plan to be quiet, restful, and helpful. Ask Him to soften your face and to sweeten your voice, to enrich your entire inner life, and He will do it.

Take time to pray. Take time to be alone with God. Learn the art of being still. Find joy in solitude. Learn to love quietness. Look up all God says about silence, quietness, and being still. Bring your soul into calmness.

Love Never Fails

As we walk in love, we walk in the light of faith. As we walk in this light, we cannot fail. There is no failure in the love life. Failure comes from selfishness.

As we walk in love, we walk in the light of His Word. There is continually a sense of God's protection and care. *"The LORD is my light and my salvation; whom shall I fear? The LORD is the strength of my life; of whom shall I be afraid?"* (Psalm 27:1).

As long as you walk in love, you are in the light. When you are walking in the light, you will not stumble. There is a fearless certainty about your life, about your decisions, and about everything else connected with your life.

You can confidently rest in the Word that says, *"Fear not, for I am with you"* (Isaiah 41:10). God is with you. God is in you. God is the strength of your life. You cannot be sick. You cannot be weak. You cannot be ignorant of His will. You know what His mind is, because He is imparting to you Himself, His ability.

He whispers, *"Fear not, for I am with you; be not dismayed, for I am your God"* (Isaiah 41:10). He means, "I am your Father God, your Lover, your Protector, and your Caretaker." It is easy to cast every care and anxiety upon Him. It is easy to rest in Him with a fearless joy.

He continues, *"I will strengthen you, yes, I will help you, I will uphold you with My righteous right hand"* (Isaiah 41:10). Never has righteousness been so beautiful. God's righteousness is upholding us. God's righteousness is making us fearless. God's righteousness is making us conquerors, overcomers, and victors in every fight.

Now, we can put up a solid front to the world. Now, we can enjoy His fullness. We know now that we are what He says we are, and we rejoice in it.

Try a Little Kindness

K indness is a part of God's nature. *"But You are God, ready to pardon, gracious and merciful, slow to anger, abundant in kindness"* (Nehemiah 9:17). Since you are now a new creature in Christ and His nature is in you, kindness should be a part of your new nature.

God will enable you to be kind to others, *"tenderhearted, forgiving one another, just as God in Christ forgave you"* (Ephesians 4:32). He will enable you to be patient with young people and understanding of the impetuousness of youth. He will enable you to show kindness to the elderly and to be sympathetic with those in the hospital by visiting them and showing your concern. You can show kindness to those behind prison bars, fulfilling Jesus' command to visit those in prison.

"Add to your faith virtue, to virtue knowledge,... to godliness brotherly kindness, and to brotherly kindness love" (2 Peter 1:5, 7). Show friendliness and kindness, generosity and courtesy, to your brothers

and sisters in Christ. *"As we have opportunity, let us do good to all, especially to those who are of the household of faith"* (Galatians 6:10).

You can show kindness and long-suffering to those who are victims of alcoholism, seeking to lead them to Jesus and His deliverance. *"Love suffers long and is kind"* (1 Corinthians 13:4). *"Therefore, as the elect of God, holy and beloved, put on tender mercies, kindness, humility, meekness, longsuffering"* (Colossians 3:12).

Many people tend to shun the mentally ill. Yet, statistics show that every other hospital bed is occupied by a person who is mentally ill. They, more than anyone, need our affectionate concern. Jesus' love compels us to have compassion on them and pray for their deliverance.

Show Christian love and kindness to those who have been overtaken in sin. Do not assume a holier-than-thou attitude, but be humble, realizing that such could happen to you but for the grace of God. Jesus showed love and compassion to the woman found guilty of adultery, and we are constrained by His example to show such compassion to others.

Blessed be the LORD, for He has shown me His marvelous kindness in a strong city!
(Psalm 31:21)

For His merciful kindness is great toward us. "For the mountains shall depart and the hills be removed, but My kindness shall not depart from you…," says the LORD, who has mercy on you.

(Isaiah 54:10)

The love of Christ that dwells within you will enable you to be kind and sympathetic toward others, gracious and friendly, benevolent toward the less privileged, and congenial in all your relationships.

The Ministry of Believers

Recently, my heart has been deeply moved. I have seen that a group of men and women who will recognize the absolute lordship of Jesus Christ over their lives will become invincible.

There are three things that need to be emphasized: first, the lordship of Jesus Christ; second, the lordship of love, the Jesus kind of love; and third, the fellowship with Jesus Christ in carrying out the Great Commission and the sharing of burdens with one another.

The Lordship of Jesus

The lordship of Jesus solves every single problem of life. If He is your Lord, then you are no longer bearing burdens for yourself. You may bear the burdens of others, but you have none, for He is your Lord.

If you have a business problem, He is your partner. You can sit down quietly with Him in the morning for a few moments and get His mind for the day. His Word becomes the absolute Lord of your life.

No matter what your vocation, He is a part of it. You are but carrying out His will in it. His will utterly governs you. You study the Word until His mind dominates your mind, for the New Testament is the mind of Christ. He becomes your ability to meet every problem.

If He is your Lord, then He is your righteousness. He is the strength of your life. He is your ability for every contingency that may arise. The lordship of Jesus is the key to success. The lordship of Jesus is the key to joy, rest, and quietness of spirit.

The Lordship of Love

Jesus brought a new kind of love to the world. He said,

> *A new commandment I give to you, that you love one another; as I have loved you, that you also love one another. By this all will know that you are My disciples, if you have love for one another.* (John 13:34–35)

This love displaces every other force that governs human life. It is the very nature of God engulfing, enfolding, and overwhelming us. It is the very nature of God dominating us, imparting itself to our spirits.

How gripping is a message born of love! What a mastery it gives us over the lives of other men and women. How hungry they become as they listen. Their hearts become hungry for this love.

We have a power for which they are hungry. We have an ability that they crave. We have a mastery that they have sought for all their lives. We have found it; they are still searching.

This love gives us leadership. When I love until selfishness has utterly dissolved and gone, I feel the power of it. There is a grip in it; there is a fire that glows and throbs until men say, "How he loves! God help me to love, too."

You cannot see men's weaknesses. You cannot see their failings. You cannot see their wrongs. You never think of weakness. You look at them with Jesus' eyes. You speak to them with Jesus' lips. You lay hands on them with Jesus' hands. With Jesus' feet, you go to minister to them. With Jesus' words, you set them free. With Jesus' words, you anoint them and empower them with a ministry of love.

There is nothing that the world needs as much as this. Love makes you a brother to all men. They may not know your language, but they know love's language. They may not understand your words, but they understand love.

The world will respond to love. It does not respond to selfishness. Love melts them. The church will respond. The youth of the land will respond. The elderly will melt under love, even if coldness and bitterness have gained the mastery.

Oh, men and women, can't you see that the lordship of Jesus lets Him into your life to rule it, and that the lordship of love lets love itself melt and blend and enrich every life? That is the secret of it.

Fellowship with Christ and Burden Bearing

Absolute fellowship is the ultimate result of redemption. This was the dream that God had for Adam. God created the world and man with one dream; that dream was marred and broken, and God was robbed of fellowship with His people.

Now, God has called us into fellowship with His Son, Jesus Christ, to save a lost world and to rejuvenate a broken church. He has called us into fellowship, burden bearing, and sharing our best with the broken and discouraged.

We bring our treasure of love. Mary brought the oil of spikenard and poured it upon the feet of Jesus. (See John 12:1–3.) Today, we pour our service, mellowed with love, upon the weary, discouraged, and broken.

We go down to the level of the broken human being, just as Jesus became identified with man, came to his level, and partook of flesh and blood so that He might become one with us. In the same way, we go down to the level of the diseased, outcast world, and we take on their sorrows and weaknesses. We weep over their sins.

We have the vision. We see the Christ. We fellowship with them. We have victory!

The Victory of Song

I have heard the story of a woman from Glasgow, Scotland, who one night was gazing reflectively into the murky waters of the river Clyde. The darkness of the night seemed to press down into her very soul, reminding her of the ugliness of her own life of sin.

As she stood by the edge of the water on the ferry steps, she was suddenly gripped by a desire to plunge into the river and end her bitter life. But she trembled as she heard a clear, strong voice from above singing, "There is a fountain filled with blood."

She listened, spellbound. She would wait, she decided, until the song was finished. Another voice joined in, and the words of the next stanza rushed into her heart with a new hope.

The dying thief rejoiced to see
That fountain in his day;
And there have I, though vile as he,
Washed all my sins away.

Gripped by this message, the woman dashed up the ferry steps to ask the singers if this One about whom they were singing could help her. Eagerly, she listened as they pointed her to Christ. The woman's wasted life was changed to a fruitful life of service to the Lord.

This woman became a successful servant of God in the slums of Glasgow. God worked through a song of testimony to reach this destitute soul. She was converted, and, in turn, she was used of the Lord to help the lost find peace, forgiveness, and victory in Jesus.

Truly, singing the praise and testimony of God is one of our instruments of power! Thank God for the beautiful inspiration and spiritual liberation of Christian singing. There is victory in song. *"Let the saints be joyful in glory; let them sing aloud on their beds. Let the high praises of God be in their mouth, and a two-edged sword in their hand"* (Psalm 149:5–6). This is real, bold Bible living to cultivate the singing heart!

The world has perverted song to purposes of evil passion, turning song into one of the most alluring agencies of temptation. But when we are converted, the Lord does some wonderful things for us. As David said,

He also brought me up out of a horrible pit, out of the miry clay, and set my feet upon a rock, and established my steps. **He has put a new**

song in my mouth; praise to our God; many will see it and fear, and will trust in the Lord.
(Psalm 40:2–3, emphasis added)

I can hardly emphasize enough the great victory there is in song—in singing the praises of the Lord. There is a real release and therapy in singing songs of spiritual liberation, songs of testimony, and songs about the Lord's power and keeping. *"They sang praises with gladness, and they bowed their heads and worshiped"* (2 Chronicles 29:30).

In the book of Ezra, the author describes how the people sang and praised the Lord with great joy. (See Ezra 3:10–13.) This gladness and joy in their singing and praising was their strength. (See Nehemiah 8:10.) From this singing, they derived spiritual and mental health to rebuild the temple and the city of Jerusalem. Indeed, they were strong and confident because of the song in their mouths.

Maintaining a Singing Heart

Heartfelt singing is charged with divine power. There is victory in song! There are two primary secrets to maintaining a singing heart: (1) be full of the Word, and (2) be full of the Spirit.

1. Be full of the Word. *"Let the word of Christ dwell in you richly in all wisdom, teaching and admonishing one another in psalms and hymns and*

spiritual songs, singing with grace in your hearts to the Lord" (Colossians 3:16).

When you are full of the Word, it produces a bold, glad song. Confessing the Word aloud will bring forth an anthem of praise. When troubles come, learn to go at them with song. When griefs arise, sing them down. Praise God by singing; that will lift you above trials of every sort.

I remember a time when I faced a very severe test. It seemed that it would crush my spirit and bring me to frustrating defeat. The need was a financial one; I was going to lose my car by repossession.

I boldly began to affirm, *"My God shall supply all your need according to His riches in glory by Christ Jesus"* (Philippians 4:19). I kept it up for about fifteen minutes, confessing it aloud over and over again. In time, that became a real song in my mouth and in my heart. I resisted the temptation to doubt by singing praises unto God. As I held my heart steady by singing, the Lord worked miraculously on my behalf and supplied the need!

Being full of the Word will cause you to sing with grace in your heart to the Lord.

2. Be full of the Spirit. *"Do not be drunk with wine, in which is dissipation; but be filled with the Spirit, speaking to one another in psalms and hymns*

and spiritual songs, singing and making melody in your heart to the Lord, giving thanks always for all things to God the Father in the name of our Lord Jesus Christ" (Ephesians 5:18–20).

The Spirit-filled life, lived in the bold radiance of the Spirit, is truly wonderful. "I will sing with the spirit, and I will also sing with the understanding" (1 Corinthians 14:15). When you are controlled by the Spirit, He invariably inspires much song from your heart.

Every great move of the Spirit in history was characterized by bold, gallant singing. What did Israel do when God delivered them from Egypt with a mighty hand?

> Then Moses and the children of Israel sang this song to the LORD…."The LORD is my strength and song, and He has become my salvation; He is my God, and I will praise Him; my father's God, and I will exalt Him."
> (Exodus 15:1–2)

What produced one of the most unusual interventions of God in the New Testament?

> At midnight Paul and Silas were praying and singing hymns to God, and the prisoners were listening to them. Suddenly there was a great earthquake, so that the foundations of the prison were shaken; and immediately all the doors

were opened and everyone's chains were loosed.
(Acts 16:25–26)

Our circumstances may be dismal at times, and we may deplore the troubles besetting us, but our difficulties are usually mild compared to those of Paul and Silas. Their backs had been beaten to ribbons, and they had been thrust into that dirty, dark, inner dungeon with their feet fast in the stocks.

However, these men were the righteous of the Lord, as bold as lions, who could sing praises to God even under such circumstances. God intervened for them, and He will intervene for us if we demonstrate such loving confidence and bold faith in our God to praise Him in song, even when everything around us cries out, "Defeat!"

There is no defeat to the bold Christian who sings God's praises, saying, "*Thanks be to God who always leads us in triumph in Christ*" (2 Corinthians 2:14), or, "*Serve the LORD with gladness; come before His presence with singing*" (Psalm 100:2).

God delights in your songs to Him. Whether you have the talent to sing or not, you are singing best when it is unto the Lord! Such song has wonderful power to banish gloom, to quicken your spirit, and to inspire you to bold courage for living in an age when God's way of life is being pushed aside by Satan.

In heaven, we shall be a singing people. And here on earth, we should keep our hearts drawn heavenward by singing. Fill your home with song; teach your children to sing. Sing as you travel to and from work, or as you work about the house. Songs of praise to Jesus can go with us wherever God leads us as we walk boldly in Him. Words in songs are words that work wonders!

A Promoter of Praise

I shall never forget my experience on the Netherlands Antilles island called Saba. Arriving on the small island was a unique experience. Pastor Williams of the Wesleyan Holiness Church met us at the airport and took us immediately up a steep mountain that came winding down into several villages until we arrived at the capital city.

Ministering there in Saba was a delight. It was during a singing service that the Holy Spirit spoke a clear word to me that has remained with me throughout my years of ministry. The Sabans were singing with inspiration the great hymn "Boundless Salvation" by William Booth:

> And now, hallelujah,
> The rest of my days
> Shall gladly be spent
> In promoting His praise!

Then, the Spirit of God spoke this to my heart: "That's your ministry. The rest of your days shall gladly be spent in promoting His praise!" I now say it unashamedly: I am a promoter of praise. And one of the most blessed ways I have found to give those praises is in the victory of song.

A friend of mine, R. C. Cunningham, wrote a beautiful description of the importance and all-inclusiveness of song:

"Songs of praise are an integral part of the Spirit-filled life—not merely on any certain day, but 365 days a year. One of the best-known songs of praise is the great 'Doxology.' One hymnologist said, 'It is doubtful if any stanza of religious poetry ever written has been so often, so universally, and so heartily sung in the worship of God as this.' The word *doxology* means a short hymn full of direct praise to God. Examine it carefully and you will see that there is great meaning and significance in every line.

"'Praise God from whom all blessings flow.' God is the fountain of everything that is good. *'Every good gift and every perfect gift is from above'* (James 1:17). If we want a blessing, our gaze should be vertical rather than horizontal.

"'Praise Him, all creatures here below.' In the last half of Psalm 148, the Scripture summons the creatures of the sea, the lightning, the mountains and forests, the beasts and the birds to unite with all ranks and ages of men and women in giving homage and praise to their Creator. The purpose of all creation is to render praise to God, and this purpose will eventually be filled. Blessed are they who do it here and now, voluntarily.

"'Praise Him above, ye heavenly host.' Not only the angels, but also the sun and moon, the heavens, and all the '*stars of light*' are called to participate in the doxology of the universe. (See Psalm 148:1–6.)

"'Praise Father, Son, and Holy Ghost.' The Father loves us, the Son redeems us, and the Spirit enlivens us. Surely we have abundant cause to praise the Holy Trinity!"

Don't Lose Your Song

Have you lost your song? Perhaps the songs we have been referring to have become clogged up in your life. Many times, people allow the cares of the world to weigh them down.

The Bible tells us that when Hezekiah, the good king of Judah, cleaned up the house of the Lord, repaired the altar, and commanded the burnt offering to be made, "*the song of the LORD also began*" (2 Chronicles 29:27).

Perhaps you have thought your life was confined to mournful, monotonous music. But God has cheery flutes and soothing harps for you to play. Get in tune with God! Harmonize with heaven! It may require some drastic action on your part to break the discords that you have played for so long. But, in good time, you will break forth in a bright new

277

tune that will be pleasing to God, will give a lift to your life, and will begin to inspire others to change their tunes!

"*Oh, sing to the* LORD *a new song! For He has done marvelous things; His right hand and His holy arm have gained Him the victory*" (Psalm 98:1). Dare to play a different tune! The Word of God will supply you with the loveliest notes.

Faith's Love Song

Psalm 23 is a love song. It is faith's love song. It shows the quiet confidence of long associations. It shows a raptness and simplicity of faith that is thrilling.

"*The LORD is my shepherd*" (verse 1). He is my Shepherd, my Lover, my Caretaker, and my Protector. The very word *shepherd* suggests protection and care.

"*I shall not want*" (verse 1). That is confidence in the Shepherd. I shall not lack or want for any good thing. I shall not want for food, I shall not want for clothes, I shall not want for shelter, and I shall not want for health, for He is the strength of my life.

"*He makes me to lie down*" (verse 2). This is quietness, security, and rest. If there were enemies, I could not lie down. I would have to stand on guard. But He is my protection now. My Shepherd Lord shields me from the enemy.

"*In green pastures*" (verse 2). Here is the causation power of love. The picture is vivid: the clover is up to the knees; its luscious beauty charms the eye and satisfies the hungry sheep that feed.

"*He leads me beside the still waters*" (verse 2). These are gentle waters of stillness and quietness. How the heart needs quietness in these troubled days. Every anxiety and care has been cast upon Him. We are as free as children. By the side of the stream, we rest in security.

"*He restores my soul*" (verse 3). This is a picture of one who has become filled with anxiety and fear until he is on the verge of a nervous collapse. Yet God restores the troubled, restless, unhappy mind to a normal condition. This is one of the most beautiful facts connected with this divine care.

When you know that He cares for you and that you have cast every anxiety upon Him, it leaves you fresh and happy to do your work. The one burdened with anxiety can't do much. The Father intends that we should trust Him with utter abandon. It is love's trust; it is love's fearlessness.

"*He leads me in the paths of righteousness for His name's sake*" (verse 3). This is one of the rarest privileges of this wonderful life—to be guided into the realm of righteousness, into the place where you can stand in the Father's presence without a sense of inferiority or of guilt.

How few have allowed the Shepherd to guide them in the paths of righteousness! How few have ever had the unique, unspeakable privilege of fellow-shipping with the Father and carrying out His will in the earth. You see, when you know this, you can do the work that Jesus left unfinished of healing the sick, feeding the multitudes, comforting the broken-hearted, and actually walking in His footsteps.

And notice that He leads you in the paths of righteousness "*for His name's sake.*" That means the use of the name of Jesus, the name that has all authority on earth, the name that rules demons and heals diseases, the name that brings health, strength, and comfort to the hearts of men.

Remember that Jesus said, "*When He, the Spirit of truth, has come, He will guide you into all truth*" (John 16:13). The Holy Spirit has come and is now waiting to guide each Christian into the truth of the finished work of Christ, the truth of righteousness, the truth of using Jesus' name, and the truth of the Father's love and care. Oh, if only righteousness became truth in our lives, even to a few of the members of the body of Christ, we could shake the world!

"*Yea, though I walk through the valley of the shadow of death, I will fear no evil; for You are with me*" (verse 4). Here is the fearless walk through the realm of spiritual death, surrounded by the forces of darkness, living among those who have only sensory knowledge, where demons rule the majority.

Yet this is the sweetest and gladdest walk that's known. You can boldly praise God and say, "Yea, though I walk where death faces me everywhere, I will not fear." You are no longer afraid of disease and sickness, no longer afraid of want and need; you are trusting in the Lord with utter abandon, resting upon His Word with a sure confidence.

With the sense of His presence, the consciousness of His faithfulness, you know that fear has been destroyed and faith has won the mastery. Jesus' promise, "*I am with you always, even to the end of the age*" (Matthew 28:20), has become a living reality. I know of nothing that can mean more to believers than to have the consciousness of His presence with them all the time.

"*Your rod and Your staff, they comfort me*" (verse 4). The Word and His fellowship are priceless gifts to man today. This living Word and the illumination of the Spirit upon it make life complete.

"*You prepare a table before me in the presence of my enemies*" (verse 5). This is feasting. You do not eat in the presence of enemies; you eat with joy only in the presence of friends. Something must have happened to your enemies for you to have a table spread in their presence. The enemies have been conquered. They can no longer injure your heart. The enemies may have been doubt, fear, or a hundred other infirmities, but they are conquered.

"*You anoint my head with oil*" (verse 5). Only two classes are anointed: royalty and the priesthood. You are in the royal family, for your Father God is

King. You are also in the royal priesthood to minister and to show forth the praises of Him who called you out of darkness into His marvelous light. (See 1 Peter 2:9.) The anointing oil of the Spirit is upon you. You are prepared for ministry—the limitless ministry of the God-indwelt, the God-led, and the God-empowered.

"My cup runs over" (verse 5). Instead of need and want, you have reached affluence. You have enough for yourself and others. Your cup is like the widow's jar of oil. (See 2 Kings 4:1–7.) The more you pour out, the more you have. The more you give, the more you possess. The overflowing cup is the cup of blessing.

"Surely goodness and mercy shall follow me all the days of my life" (verse 6). These are the traits of love, goodness, and loving-kindness, and they keep company with you from morning until night. They watch by the bedside.

"And I will dwell in the house of the LORD forever" (verse 6). This is fellowship of the highest order. This is the consummation of redemption. This is the culmination of life's dream.

About the Authors

E. W. Kenyon

Born in Saratoga county, New York, E. W. Kenyon (1867–1948) moved with his family to Amsterdam, New York, when he was in his teens. Kenyon studied at Amsterdam Academy and, at the age of nineteen, preached his first sermon in the Methodist church there.

He worked his way through school, attending various schools in New Hampshire, as well as Emerson College in Boston, Massachusetts.

Kenyon served as pastor of several churches in the New England states. At the age of thirty, he founded and became president of Bethel Bible Institute in Spencer, Massachusetts. (This school was later moved to Providence, Rhode Island, and is known as Providence Bible Institute.) Through his ministry at Bethel, hundreds of young men and women were trained and ordained for the ministry.

After traveling throughout the Northeast preaching the gospel and seeing the salvation and healing of thousands, Kenyon moved to California, where he continued his evangelistic travels. He was pastor of a church in Los Angeles for several years and was one of the pioneers of radio work on the Pacific Coast.

In 1931, he moved to the Northwest, and for many years his morning broadcast, *Kenyon's Church of the Air,* was an inspiration and blessing to thousands. He also founded the New Covenant Baptist Church in Seattle, where he pastored for many years.

During the busy years of his ministry, he found time to write and publish sixteen books, as well as many correspondence courses and tracts, and he composed hundreds of poems and songs. The work that he started has continued to bless untold thousands.

Don Gossett

For more than fifty years, Don Gossett has been serving the Lord through full-time ministry. Born again at the age of twelve, Don answered his call to the ministry just five years later, beginning by reaching out to his unsaved family members. In March 1948, Don overcame his longtime fear of public speaking and began his ministry in earnest, preaching for two country Baptist churches in Oklahoma.

Blessed with the gift of writing, Don became editor of the Bible College magazine in San Francisco;

afterward, he was invited to become editor of an international magazine. Following this, he served as editor of T. L. Osborn's *Faith Digest*, a magazine that reached over 600,000 homes each month. Don apprenticed with many well-known evangelists, beginning with William Freeman, one of America's leading healing evangelists during the late 1940s. He also spent time with Jack Coe and Raymond T. Richey.

Don has penned many works, particularly ones on the power of the spoken word and praise. His writings have been translated into almost twenty languages and have exceeded twenty-five million in worldwide distribution. Additionally, Don has also recorded scores of audio series. His daily radio broadcast, launched in 1961, has been released into eighty-nine nations worldwide.

Don raised five children with his first wife, Joyce, who died in 1991. In 1995, Don found lifelong love again and married Debra, an anointed teacher of the Word. They have ministered worldwide and have lived in British Columbia, Canada, and in Blaine, Washington State.